LIVING GRIEF

A MOTHER/S ODYSSEY OF SURRENDER, RENEWAL, AND MAD JOY

ANGELINA AVEDANO, PHD

ISBN: 978-1-950186-27-3

Author email: dr.aavedano@gmail.com
Author website: cycada.squarespace.com

Cover and interior design by Jennifer Leigh Selig
Cover art by Karen Ohnesorge
Author photo by Anthony DeAngelis of Angel's Eyes Portraiture

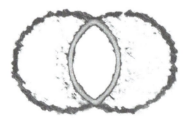

MANDORLA BOOKS
WWW.MANDORLABOOKS.COM

DEDICATION

For Thom

Your name I did not change, because you help me remember the one thing that remains.

TABLE OF CONTENTS

ACKNOWLEDGMENTS

I owe a debt of gratitude to my sons who have undertaken this lifelong odyssey with me without consent. My hope is that they will benefit from my developing awareness in ways as yet unknown. To my husband, whose unwavering belief in my work makes it possible for me to embrace what comes with mad joy, thank you. Profound thanks to my teacher and guide, Thom, who held the mirror gently but firmly all these years. I am indebted to my mentor and champion Dennis Patrick Slattery for gracing this project with an enchanting Foreword. My love and respect to the many teachers who opened doors and provided keys: Joseph, John, Deanna, and Karen (whose artwork exquisitely evokes the emotion of this project). To my collaborators and conspirators in the sacred circle that nurtured the seeds: Kayden, Stephanie, and Jaffa (my dear "midwife" and guide). My deepest gratitude to the broken-hearted who shared themselves with raw honesty and courage: Jen, Constantia, and Bonnie. To the brother I never had, Philip, thank you for everything. To Jennifer Selig, for guidance, and making it happen. I want to honor those who encouraged, challenged, instigated, and inspired—Becky C, Lisa D, Sharon O, Rachel D, and Heather M. To Cheryl, who intuitively knew which books to share; I wish you were here. Thanks to my loving mother for the meticulous red-lining (and reading this in its most unpolished, verbose, and impenetrable state. I'm so sorry!). To my forever-daughter Courtney, who nourishes my soul in countless ways. Thank you Jelani, Rachelle, and Bob, who tend to my health and well-being. To my mythological guides who pointed the way; and for the whispers, consoling words, and nudges from so many who remain unnamed—my heart is full because of you. Finally, I must express my eternal gratitude to the father of my sons, without whom this journey would not have begun.

FOREWORD

In the Texas Hill Country where I live, the drought this summer has been extensive and intense. Our home is located midway between San Antonio to the south and Austin to the north. Every other morning I start early to water a handful of bushes, trees, and shrubs in an attempt to keep them from dying. The rest of the 5.5 acres has to fend for itself, which it does in its own natural way.

Many of the smaller trees have shed their leaves in late September, much earlier than usual. Bushes are turning brown. The grass has not needed cutting since mid-May and we have not had a good rain on our property since at least then. Now we are well into October and the temperature is still in the mid-90s. But I had more in mind than beginning this Foreword by simply offering a dire weather report.

What I have been noticing is how nature protects herself when there is not enough moisture: it begins to die, or gives the impression and appearance of expiration. The grass is a light tan, several of the trees are barren and the Texas Lilac bushes are turning brown to join in the drought medley. Their stasis is their preservation so they can renew when it rains or remain quiescent until early spring. I know they appreciate the occasional hose watering, but they have taken matters into their own hands. They have descended into hibernation early in order to bloom with new life next year.

I think the above description is an apt and rich metaphor for Angelina's story, which details her own dormancy, feelings of deep depression, and a death descent into herself as she deals year after year with her son Steven's schizophrenic disorder—his remaining silent for months, then suddenly surfacing, her constant self-scrutiny and self-laceration over what else she might have done in raising him to spare him and her family the suffering wrought by such a mental illness, and the erratic behavior that often grows from its soil. At one point I began to consider how Angelina uses her knowledge, her compassion, and her elegant word choices as a means of descending into the Underworld of her and her son's suffering in order to survive it and the drought that it carries to all members in the home.

They fold in on themselves, preserve their energy, go dormant, and become solitary in order to preserve themselves from the violence of scarcity. So it has been for Angelina. In her convertible ride accompanied by Rod Stewart's *Forever Young*, she learns, toward the end of her memoir, to cooperate with what is rather than warring against her son Steven's illness as well as the system that he is both ensnared in and helped by. She learns to die in order to live, as the greenery on our property is struggling to do. Like Angelina, the trees and plants are grieving and grounding themselves so to sustain, not die, to life.

I might add here that given the horrific pandemic the world, and especially the United States is going through today, there is a corollary to Angelina's story. For she has gone through personally what has gone viral in the collective psyche of humanity in its collective global presence. The level of grieving in the United States as I write this, with over 10 million infected and approaching 250,000 dead, is unprecedented and beyond the ability to be recorded. As a species, we are grieving within the archetype of the Mother/s Odyssey.

Moreover, Angelina's painful narrative reveals many seasons of dying, with Steven cycling in and out of her life, hospitals, arrests and jails. At one point Angelina went six years without seeing him. In some compassionate and selfless synchronicity with her son, she has a revelation that her dreams of his recovery "had to die too." In such a grief and guilt-laden journey, she feels asphyxiated at many crossroads by what she calls "the dark mother," who is (s)mothering, suffocating, and merciless. Angelina recognizes, as her own anguish, feelings of guilt and shame continuing to rise in the thermostat of her struggles with Steven, that her suffering in "May and June of 2018 was not about the life of my son, it was about my death—the death of the good mother."

But the texture of her narrative goes far beyond her own and Steven's to embrace what Angelina has loved, teaches, and learns from: the realm of myth, legend, fairy tales, and literary classics. To name only a few, we read about Anticlea, the mother of Odysseus, who tells her son when he visits her in the Underworld, that she died of grief over the loss of him in her life. We also meet Demeter and Persephone, Pentheus, Hera, Inanna, Artemis and Actaeon, Shiva, Sethe and Paul D. from Toni

Morrison's novel *Beloved*, and so many others. Angelina's story gains a rich yeast from these mythic and imaginal figures from the past, but who are actually palpably present in the imaginations of so many people today.

These characters serve Angelina to widen and deepen her perspective on her own journey of suffering, not, however, devoid of moments of joy and wonder in her own life and that of her sons, for Steven has siblings that are presences in his life as well. She rightly reveals that there is implicit in these literary and mythic figures' stories deep analogies to her narrative; through them, she writes, "I am able to find forgiveness for myself, for my son, and for the institutions that have wounded both of us over the years." We might recall here the insight of the analyst and mythologist C. G. Jung, who writes that "analogy formation is a law which to a large extent governs the life of the psyche." For Angelina, creating rich analogies of her plight is redemptive and renewing.

Such enduring and often endearing stories offer deep corridors of clarity for our lives and help us, as they guide Angelina's quest to express through memories that often exhaust her, the underlying patterns that are universal, human, and comforting when we put our own narratives beside their poetic brilliance. They offer her another way of knowing, a mythic sensibility that uncovers, even unlocks parts of her telling that she may never have seen without them. These eternal stories are a balm, even *a salve to the soul* that has been tattered by suffering and longing, tragic and lyric, with moments of comic interludes.

No less is the act of writing another salvific way of encountering what feels like it cannot be survived: "Writing is my way of navigating the abundance of emotion I carry" she writes, "as well as the perpetual grief inherent in the Mother/s Odyssey. Writing is where I discover the most authentic sense of myself." The image that follows is one of the most arresting in its dramatic intensity: "Penning letters to my son feels like throwing pieces of my soul over the edge of a cliff."

It would not be surprising to learn from her that writing this history of her life with Steven as she navigates a marriage in distress, her other sons' needs, her teaching obligations, and her writing, has had a similar dismembering effect, wherein life itself continues to gnaw around the edges of her courage, attempting to dispel any sense of unity and coherence of a life in need of re-composition.

The end of her story begins in hope and a shifted perspective on her life's plotline. Enter Rod Stewart's song, the convertible and a joyful feeling of renewal:

> By facing what I had spent decades avoiding, controlling, and suppressing—something shifted. For the first time, I now have joy in a way that I previously could not. I did not plan for it or expect it; but, my newly discovered joy is evident every day. It is not joy in spite of grieving; this mad joy, like a lotus, emerges out of the murky depths of perpetual grief.

This last insight is an epic moment in her life and her relationship with Steven. He has been the obstacle that became an opening for her to more fully accept her own limits, liabilities, and love for herself through the love for her broken and heroic son. Indeed, it is not a story to pass on, but to live through with the level of passion in which it is expressed.

Dennis Patrick Slattery, Ph.D.
Distinguished Professor Emeritus in Mythological Studies,
Pacifica Graduate Institute, and author of *Riting Myth, Mythic Writing: Plotting Your Personal Story*, and *From War to Wonder: Recovering Your Personal Myth Through Homer's Odyssey*

PREFACE

This is not a book only for mothers. It is meant for those who have experienced profound grief no matter what form it takes. This powerful emotion naturally occurs in response to the death of a loved one. However, other losses too inspire grief—a loss of faith, an aspect of one's identity, a beloved pet, or a cherished, irreplaceable memento. The loss of one's health for example, or more specifically, the loss of a breast, a bone, memory, or cognition can instigate deep sorrow as well. When in the grips of profound grief, we are brought low. It feels as if we cannot go on. We are propelled into the depths of the soul on our grief passage; this is what I call the "Mother Odyssey."

Since my aim is to include a broad spectrum of grief encounters, the Mother Odyssey needs to expand beyond a mother's loss, which is why I adopted Elisabeth Schüssler Fioreza's forward slash in the spelling of "A Mother/s Odyssey." She uses the forward slash to create the inclusive term "wo/man," wherein male and female coexist, rather than excluding the feminine by using "man" or "men" as generic. In similar fashion, a "Mother/s" Odyssey signifies the variety of experiences that set the grief passage in motion. Profound loss is not necessarily related to the loss of a child, but collectively, human consciousness recognizes the enormity of a mother's grief and understands this as an extreme emotional trauma. Furthermore, I am using this spelling to denote the primal (original, elemental, and intrinsic) quality of profound grief. With rare exceptions, a Mother/s Odyssey is a journey every human being will face.

Living Grief: A Mother/s Odyssey of Surrender, Renewal, and Mad Joy explores the nature of loss, as well as the cycles of grief. Of course, there are aspects of memoir in telling such a personal story, but more than that, this is a mythological approach to grief that emphasizes the potential for transformation. As one passes through a period of tremendous loss, the grief passage becomes a primal human endeavor that elicits personal growth. This "odyssey" is a process of descent and return—and profound grief is the "mother" of all odysseys. Anyone who has experienced such a journey or who is currently enduring their grief passage knows the abyss of sorrow into which we descend, that barren place where we face the darkest parts of ourselves. In desperation, we seek out the stories of others to help us make sense of our own. Myths and stories help to redefine grief by reimagining loss as a catalyst. In this way, a mythological reading of grief offers a new perspective, one infused with possibilities. Looking at a variety of myths and stories about grief is what enabled me to find meaning in the meaningless of my son's schizophrenia, and to reimagine what it meant to be a grieving mother.

Although it is a basic human emotion, grief often disrupts our sense of self, causing us to question our faith and lose hope, because it challenges the way we see the world and ourselves in it. However, it can also inspire—helping us to focus, to cull out of our lives unhealthy behaviors, self-sabotage, and distractions. Grief causes us to take stock of what matters and to reevaluate our choices. As such, the Mother/s Odyssey is an undertaking that drives us to new depths, dragging us through the muck toward what would seem to be our annihilation.

Even as I write this, our global community has been thrust into a collective grief passage. Our entire way of life has been upended by a virus, a virus and the repercussions which will be with us indefinitely. Now more than ever, it is imperative that we engage with grief, understand its ways, and tap into its potential. On a collective level, we are experiencing now what every grieving soul has endured. Much of what we have come to depend on, our worldviews, our sense of stability, is under threat. Not only are we facing the very real and frightening prospect of physical death because of a pandemic, we are grappling with the death of our world as we have known it. Around the globe, individuals are reeling, trying to orient themselves to emerging cataclysmic changes—social, economic, and environmental. Add to this the trauma of reopening and examining deep racial wounds, and we have no choice but to confront the realities of profound grief. Many are feeling this enormous collective grief along with their own. Therefore, we now have an opportunity to understand grief on a more personal level, and carry that new understanding toward our next inevitable encounter with loss.

Along the course of a Mother/s Odyssey, initially, we are stripped of any notion of security.[1] What is familiar becomes foreign, and we remain in this state of trauma for as long as we must. There is no willing it away or rushing the process; and yet, once the grief passage is underway, we eventually learn to adapt and to recognize its cycles. When we allow these cycles to pass naturally without resisting them, we find ourselves transformed. We are no longer martyred by despair, no longer governed by a desire to control outcomes and circumstances, no longer enslaved by expectations. Instead, by some strange paradox, the one who grieves is held in tension, suspended somewhere between surrender and liberation. Our grieving souls hover there, ever-shifting from one pole to the next—from hope to despair and back again. However, this very oscillation is one of the enduring characteristics of the grief passage; it is that which initiates our metamorphosis.

Another characteristic of the Mother/s Odyssey, is the "living" nature of this complex emotion. What is "living" or "perpetual" grief? It is an ongoing relationship with loss; it is something we carry, a soul wound—and the inevitable catalyst for our metamorphosis. We are transformed by the Mother/s Odyssey when we learn to surrender to our cruel mistress. For she possesses the key to our survival. Living grief teaches us to let go of the idea that surrender is a sacrifice. Instead, it becomes the sacrament which breaks us out of the carapace of holding on, propelling us toward acceptance, urging us to forgive.

Forgiveness is not only offered to others, but to ourselves. My friend and mentor Dennis Patrick Slattery describes the work of forgiveness: "Certainly some outside force is needed for all of us to forgive the wounds and the wounding we do in the world."[2] Forgiveness is essential to transformation, because it allows one to release emotions that are unproductive. Releasing or "letting go" is an ongoing practice of reverent acceptance. It is not something that is done once, but something to which we return time and again. Letting go is the reward in action; and it seems (as Dennis suggests) that it will take the power of the gods to realize this reward.

Yet living grief means that we carry our wounds, not as our trauma, but our triumph. I cannot promise that pain and sorrow of loss will "end" if you read this book. However, in my experience, the Mother/s Odyssey provides a new perspective on living grief, one which fuels our growth. Like everything in nature, it is a cycle. Wherever you find yourself on your grief passage, the landscape will inevitably change. Nature promises us life, death, *and* regeneration. So too it is with our hearts and souls.

~Angelina Avedano, July 2020

CHAPTER ONE

A Fool's Errand

Would it be better if he were dead? My heart recoils as it pounds mercilessly inside my head. Foreboding weighs heavy like the humid air. Dull white ceiling tiles blur, and my eyes sting as a breath catches in my chest. I am trembling, alone, and confused. This nightmarish feeling is consuming—I am disoriented and terrified. Red LEDs blink 2:00 am. I slowly realize I am trapped inside my son's mind. It is loud, chaotic, and ominous. I am bombarded by emotions, sounds, and shadows; they surge like angry flood waters. Voices, not quite audible, but oppressive and maddening, pull my attention in all directions. I cannot focus on any one voice or any one image. I am unable to anchor my thoughts, feelings, or even my sense of self. This is psychic torment like I have never experienced. As the minutes tick by, now 2:12, 2:13, 2:14, my thoughts begin to separate from the confusion. It feels as if I am untangling my psyche, prying it away from this larger, more dense and knotted mass of God knows what. My heart is beating fast, my breathing rapid and shallow as it dawns on me—this is my son's daily existence.

Steven was being held in a state-run facility on the island of Oahu. He had been ordered to undergo a psychiatric evaluation by a Honolulu county judge. A few months earlier, I was awarded a grant to participate in a summer program during the month of June at a university nearby. The program was an exciting professional opportunity, but my main objective was to see my son for the first time in over six years. With anticipation, I began my journey at Logan International Airport after a harried Boston commute, but I had no way of preparing for the emotional cyclone I would face. I was simply thankful that at the time I would be attending the summer institute on Oahu, Steven would be somewhere I could find him.

During a manic episode five years earlier, he had flown to Honolulu after seeing some brochures about Hawai'i in the window of a travel agency in Eureka, California. One day, without warning, he called: "Hey Mom, guess what? I'm in Honolulu!" At first, I didn't believe him, but disbelief was quickly replaced by panic. We had already been as far away from each other as I could imagine. At that time, I had been on the East Coast for a few years, and he was living in an apartment he acquired through disabilities' services on the West Coast. It was unthinkable that we were no longer on the same land mass. More and more, the ocean separating us was not only a psychological metaphor, but a physical reality. I would soon confront the vast expanse between his world and mine.

For over a decade, I went through several periods of time when I had no idea whether my son was alive or dead. During many dark nights, my frenzied thoughts would spiral, conjuring and catastrophizing all manner of violent scenarios. This nightmare stretched on as I was plagued by visions of Steven beaten, raped, or dead. Repeatedly, I would play out "the call" in my mind, the one informing me that his body had been found.

Most parents understand that living with this kind of fear is unsustainable. The heart and mind can only take so much. During such times, when drowning in worry and grief, I would remind myself that so many mothers and fathers had grieved their children. What would they give to sit across from their child, no matter what their condition was, just to see them and touch them again? This is what I told myself as I climbed the hill to the locked-down security wing of Steven's residence hall three to four times a week during my stay in Hawai'i. Even if the circumstances were less than ideal, my son was alive. Although my heart felt mangled and threadbare, I considered myself one of the fortunate ones.

It was the second week of the summer program at the university when I had the dream of being trapped inside Steven's mind. It was a dream, but not a dream. The myriad voices, disorganized stream of consciousness, and claustrophobia made it hard to breathe. The "noise" in my head created confusion and anxiety. Because of this strange experience, I understood the look about Steven that I would come to observe during our visits—a mixture of distracted paranoia and exhaustion. But again, I tried to comfort myself by remembering that at least I could lay eyes on my son. I could reassure myself that he was alive and "safe."

However, in my experience, knowing Steven's whereabouts was just as painful as not knowing. When he would surface after extended periods of being off the grid, I would receive heart-wrenching incoherent phone calls. In the year leading up to my journey to Hawai'i, I took many of these calls. Visions of torture plagued my son, and there seemed to be no way to comfort him. He was traumatized by threatening entities or "voices." For several months, during these calls Steven would go on and on about human trafficking and torture chambers. His speech was all but indecipherable due to heavy doses of medication. Slurred words compounded by disordered thinking made it difficult to understand what he was trying to say. From five thousand miles away, all of my emotional resources were brought to bear just to keep my hysteria in check as I tried to comprehend what my son was trying to tell me. For almost a decade, phone calls were the only lifeline between us. Now, that tenuous thread felt frayed and more and more likely to break.

During our conversations, Steven was so adamant about "trauma corpse" or "trauma courts" (I was unclear about what he was saying because his speech was so garbled), that I searched the internet trying to figure out what he meant. I discovered a graphic novel series entitled *Trauma Corps*. Had he seen them in a bookstore somewhere and incorporated them into his delusion? He was so focused on violent visions, describing in detail ugly sadistic acts, that I was afraid something terrible had happened. While I did my best to follow the maze in my son's mind, I wondered if these images and sensations were in fact emanating from inside of him. Was this the meaning of my dream?

In the sultry island air, I made my way from the dormitory to the lush mountains encircling the hospital several times a week to see Steven. It was the month of historic volcanic eruptions and evacuations on the Big Island that year—a seismic symbol of my emotional upheaval. During our visits, he would almost always speak of battling evil. He would go on long diatribes about discrimination and other systemic problems. He was passionate about social justice, devising plans to organize and raise funds to address these issues when he "got out." His rants had a certain youthful idealism, and I couldn't help but think that my tender, precocious boy was still there beneath the erratic synapses and chemical imbalances in the brain of the thirty-one-year-old man sitting before me.

Following Steven's train of thought during our conversations was exhausting. He described his "voices" as mostly sinister, but not always. Video games he played and movies he had seen throughout the years overlapped in his mind in such a way that they were part of his current reality. He told stories about encounters with celebrities like Christopher Lloyd from the movie *Back to the Future*; or he would fixate on one of his acquaintances from the past who reminded him of Eminem, whose popularity skyrocketed right around the time Steven was first hospitalized when he was thirteen. Each time, I came away from our visits feeling physically weak and emotionally spent from the energy it took to focus on and decode his monologues. One thing was clear—my son was deeply troubled and he was searching for a way to put his thoughts in order.

The most difficult part of my time with my son was my inability to comfort him. For years, I worried that he would spend his life alone. He rarely made friends as a child and that pattern continued into adulthood. Steven did not experience any real long-term relationships outside of our family, but I held out hope that he would find someone who would love him. I tried to imagine what it must be like to go for years without any compassionate human contact. During one of our visits, I reached out and placed my hand on his arm. I was hesitant because I did not know how he would respond. Would the touch of my hand feel invasive or threatening? How long had it been since anyone had touched him with love or compassion? Of course, he always greeted me with a hug, but that was different. He looked at my hand a couple times before he briefly grabbed it saying, "I love you so much, Mom." I did not dare let go, and tried to read his face for indications of emotion or clarity, but he was in another world. He would glance at me, then distractedly look away. I held back tears, because I couldn't let him see how painful it was to be there. He was sitting right in front of me, but I didn't know how to reach him through the veil of his mystifying illness.

Steven was gracious during my visits. He would say again and again that he was glad I was there, and that I always had been there for him. Although I knew he meant what he said, it was unsettling that there was no emotion to accompany his words. I assumed this was because he had been recently prescribed lithium and clozapine. I watched him struggle to eat, having to place each bite of food in line with his teeth because his tongue was paralyzed due to the meds. It became clear why he mumbled and could not form his words during those agonizing phone calls over the years. I had since learned how to interpret his speech, but seeing him now, I understood what was causing it. Steven was self-conscious about drooling as a result of impaired muscle control. His jaw rippled and I could see the tremors in his hands. His pupils were dilated so that his eyes had a strange, wide stare. Likely his meds and mental state flattened his affect and made him seem so far removed. Either way the son I remembered—the passionate musician, keen intellect, and artistic soul I loved—seemed absent.

Mothers can sense a lot about their children, even from great distances. Surely fathers can too. I have wondered whether my sons realize how much I "feel" them, how connected we are no matter where they happen to be in their lives. But in that moment, it felt as if a thick wall of sound-proof (and sensation-proof) glass stood between me and Steven. We could stare at each other, but we simply could not reach one another. Steven seemed to "see" that I was speaking to him, but he was hearing too many other voices to make out which was mine. We had developed a special bond when he was young, in large part because of the long and difficult journey we had been on since his diagnosis. This made my inability to reach him, or to free him from his captivity (or to comfort him), especially tragic.

While visiting my son in the psychiatric hospital, a sickening image would come to my mind of feeding an animal at the zoo. He asked me to bring fast food and various snacks he was unable to access otherwise. His favorites were salt and vinegar potato chips, Snickers bars, root beer, and the pièce de résistance: Arby's beef and cheddar sandwiches on onion buns. Steven would anxiously await my arrival as I cleared the vestibule after a cursory scan from a security wand, which of course was preceded by a screening at the guard shack, where I could be turned away at the charge nurse's whim when the guard called the unit to check if I was allowed to proceed. Whenever I fooled myself into thinking I had a modicum of control over any aspect of this situation, these occasions provided a harsh reminder: I was most decidedly powerless.

Even so, I filled tote bags with Steven's requested sundries and food items (all of which had to be consumed in one sitting). It was a struggle to keep track of all of the hospital rules: no caffeine, no plastic bags, no cell phone, no car keys, no hardback books. The rules were like a moving target—some things allowed one visit and not the next. My phone calls were closely governed: "Call between this time and this time." "Call back in 10 minutes." "Call back in 20 minutes." "Call back in 30 minutes." It was infuriating. Still, I knew that it could be so much worse; like the times when I would call only to find my son had been moved with no warning or discharged back on the street where I knew he would be not only off his meds, but off the grid.

Upon my arrival, Steven would be standing at the end of the hall expectantly eyeing the bags I carried. He would hug me before we were ushered into a stuffy, unpleasant little room furnished with heavy molded plastic chairs, a wooden table at one end, a bookshelf loaded with an array of paperbacks and magazines, and a rocking chair covered with a white sheet. Atlases, a tattered *Farmers' Almanac*, and several Bibles littered a sticky, wooden table. A few scouting ants were at the ready, preparing to send a signal to a nearby battalion eager to descend upon an unattended sandwich or a dribble of root beer. I faced a wall of windows, which one might think would be a respite from the stark, repulsive decor, except they were grimy and covered with filmy quarter-inch plexiglass securely screwed into the wall.

On my first visit, I was shocked by the contrast between the beauty of the bay nestled at the foot of a stunning mountain range and the oppressive appearance of the hospital looming before me. I was repulsed by a supposed "therapeutic" environment which isolated human beings from nature, as I observed outdoor "courtyards" that were actually chain-link pens surrounding cement slabs, some covered with black net. Walking toward the caged entrance of Steven's unit at the back of the hospital campus, I doubled-over in despair. I simply could not process the dissonance between the breathtaking tropical setting and the reality of my son's institutionalization.

However, after a few conversations with Steven, my perspective changed. His experience was not "my" experience. At one point, he specifically pointed out how safe he felt because of the plexiglass on the windows—he said it protected him from "evil." He let me know the hospital was a healing and safe place, the staff was kind, and he was not worried about being hurt. In fact, he expressed a desire to stay for as long as possible. Still, I struggled with my skewed interpretation of my son's situation, trying to come to terms with the fact that he felt he was not only safe, but in a good place.

Part of sorting out Steven's experience from my perception of it has been working through not only my grief but my guilt. I have sifted through my life decisions again and again, looking for explanations for why he had to suffer. For years I blamed myself—I should not have let him play video games; I should not have allowed him to play Dungeons and Dragons; I failed to shelter him from drugs and alcohol. Maybe this was why Steven had schizoaffective disorder. These rabbit holes of self-blame would cause me to obsess about his brain development. Maybe he was "damaged" *in utero*, because I was unaware I was pregnant for five months while I nursed his brother; or maybe it was because I was unable to nurse him at all. One way or another, I was sure I was responsible for my son's condition. I am not alone. When children suffer, parents not only want to prevent their suffering, they revisit every interaction and every decision, calculating all the ways they failed. Most parents relate to the extreme lengths to which we will go to protect our children; we'll make a deal with the devil to put an end to their pain.

Sadly, no amount of bargaining with the devil would change the reality of my son's illness. In my case, angels and demons were relegated to the realm of my son's mind. Sitting with him under the sterile fluorescent lights, watching him interact with "the others," my heart broke. He was immersed in animated conversations under his breath with something or someone I could not see. He paused to ask if I believed there were other dimensions, or whether I could perceive energy fields he was creating as he pointed at the floor or to the corner of the room. I explained that he was seeing and experiencing something I could not. He spoke in fits and starts about good and evil, his own magical powers, and injustices against humanity. All the while, my heart felt as if it were dissolving in my chest.

Our interactions were grounded only by whatever junk food "favorites" Steven was eating. During long periods of silence, he focused intently on the ingredients listed on the packages and closely inspected his food. He told me food spoke to him, but did not elaborate. At first, I was so taken aback by his behavior that my mind raced, looking for something that would put the situation into some kind of order. However, after my dream, I understood how draining these mental gymnastics were, because I was in full disagreement with reality. I was looking for just the right combination of words to open the lock in my son's mind, and that was a fool's errand.

The source of my agony was believing I could *do* something—*anything*—that would fix the situation. Isn't this what mothers are *supposed* to do? We protect our children, soothe their wounds, and make them "all better." But there was no making it "all better" when it came to something as powerful and debilitating as schizophrenia. Even the professionals lacked the ability to "fix" it. Psychiatrists made their best guesses, but their efforts were often trial and error at best. The judicial system, with its arbitrary lack of vision, was unable to make it better. Not that these institutions didn't at times offer help and guidance; they did. But medical and legal systems were limited in expertise when it came to the complexities of mental illness. Too often, they complicated the problem, rather than providing relief or support. Systemically, we are failing human beings like Steven; and as much as I continued to try, I worried that I was failing him, too.

CHAPTER TWO

Disintegration

When Steven was a child, I noticed little things that set him apart. I called him my "transient sleeper" because, hours after his brothers would be down for the count, he would be wide awake, never satisfied to fall asleep in the same place twice. Sometimes he would make a bed in the hall, lay underneath a table, upside-down in a chair, on a toy-box, or in a makeshift tent. That is, if I could get him to go to sleep at all. Bedtime became an ordeal, one that everyone in the house dreaded. Steven rarely went to sleep without a fight. However, it was not only my son's sleep patterns (or lack thereof) that were a hint of things to come. Looking back, there were telling signs, had I known how to read them. One thing I understood was that Steven experienced the world differently than the rest of us.

At three years old, he claimed he saw my grandfather, who had died only hours before, outside the car window. Steven's little round face pressed against the glass as he waved and smiled: "Look! There's Poppy!" I was comforted that maybe my toddler could see and experience one of the most important men in my life when I no longer could. At first, I thought maybe Steven sensed my grief, and was just trying to comfort me. Then another thought began to form. Perhaps the veil between this dimension and whatever was on the "other side" was thinner for children, especially children like Steven.

As time went on, I sensed what lay ahead, even though I couldn't admit it. One night when my son was about four years old, during a particularly difficult bedtime ritual, I asked why he could not sleep. My blood ran cold when he said people were talking to him. It would become colder still as the years went on, growing into an iceberg of sorrow.

In part because their father and I felt public school was not the best option for three rambunctious boys, but mostly due to our suspicions that it was going to be a problem for Steven, we home-schooled our sons. This worked for a couple of years, but as time went on, I was in over my head. Steven and his brothers fought constantly, always vying for attention, and looking for the kind of structure that was impossible to provide at home. Ultimately, they were enrolled in a small rural school. Around this time, my husband and I divorced and entered the chaotic years. I was briefly separated from my sons for the first time, and it took months for us to regain our footing. The trauma and lack of emotional stability made a lasting impact on all of us. Eventually, the post-divorce routine led to a somewhat "normal" life, including school plays, sports tournaments, Boy Scouts, and sleepovers.

Time went on, and Steven's fourth grade teacher was adamant that he should be tested for Attention Deficit/Hyper-activity Disorder. I resisted, convinced she was burned out and didn't have enough patience with active little boys. It was not a question of whether Steven could excel in school and social activities; in fact he thrived in creative, stimulating, hands-on surroundings. But, there were signs of looming problems, and I found myself volunteering at school, as well as extra-curricular activities, so I could head-off issues before they escalated. This strategy worked for a time.

Then puberty arrived and the spiral began. At thirteen years old, Steven was hospitalized after several disciplinary reports and a violent outburst at his middle school involving a School Resource Officer. There were several altercations between Steven and his brothers that made it impossible for them to live together, so they went to stay with their father who now lived with his new wife out of state. Steven alternated between living with me and his grandmother while we tried to figure out how to handle his impulsive behavior, unpredictable rages, and the exhausting perpetual mania.

During his first hospitalization, he was diagnosed with bipolar disorder and placed on medication; however, there was a litany of diagnoses over the coming months: bipolar disorder, conduct disorder, and oppositional defiance. Doctors assured me that these fluid diagnoses were not unusual for youth exhibiting psychiatric symptoms, since the brains of children and teens were still developing. This was because hormonal changes, food and chemical allergies or sensitivities, and experimentation with drugs and alcohol made assessing these disorders and finding appropriate treatment extremely difficult. In addition, convincing an impetuous teen that they cannot eat sweets, drink caffeine, or experiment casually with drugs and alcohol like their friends, is like trying to reason with a toddler. The more you try, the more of an issue you make of it, the more likely they are to act out. Add to this all of the emotional and behavioral challenges of being a teenager, and it is easy to understand how living with the restrictions and stigma of mental illness became devastating for Steven.

Whatever diagnosis he was facing, everyone in the family was impacted. Our other sons Travis and Devin inevitably experienced neglect while Steven's father and I tried desperately to put out fires. I became involved in support groups, searching for answers, and soon recognized that families in similar circumstances were experiencing many of the same problems. The constant emotional and financial stress took a toll on everyone. The uncertainty of each day, bracing for the next crisis, and attempting to buffer children from the consequences of their actions was overwhelming. Psychological trauma, confusion, and shame unfortunately are the lay of the land when a child is diagnosed with mental illness, and we can neither protect our families from the pain of this reality, nor the wounds we unintentionally inflict on one another.

Steven's diagnosis was not well-received by everyone in the family. I resisted putting him on antipsychotic medication, and did not want to accept what seemed to be a life sentence. It was clear however that we were running out of options. His father and others gave voice to my deepest fear: Steven would be permanently labeled "mentally ill." They believed I was overreacting to his erratic behavior, even though we were all at a loss for what to do. I was torn between wanting to maintain my relationships with Travis and Devin, and wanting to protect them from Steven's unpredictable outbursts and destructive rages, not to mention the vortex of drama that surrounded him. In truth, there were no "good" options. His brothers continued to live with their father, and I did the best I could to manage Steven's increasing needs. That was more than a full-time job. Being separated from Travis and Devin during those years shaped our relationships. I feel certain that while they were excited to go live with their father, they still felt abandoned, since all of my emotional energy was consumed by Steven's emerging mental illness. I have wrestled with this sad reality over the years, having to forgive myself, and Steven too.

Every week brought another battle, another crisis, another run-in with some authority. Around this time, Steven was caught shoplifting a bottle of hair dye at a local grocery store, which might not have been too problematic, except he was incapable of following through with the rules of the court-mandated diversion program. The rules were unforgiving, and the juvenile justice system, which had a reputation for being excessively punitive in our county, got involved.

This created even more tension between Steven's father and me, since he had little faith in the legal system and resented any invasion of privacy. I couldn't blame him; there was no dignity afforded parents in the system, with its invasive intakes, demeaning drug and alcohol programs, mandatory family counseling, and parenting classes. Even more demoralizing was the message underpinning them all—at the root of Steven's problems were all of our parental failings.

Steven's father worried that I had opened Pandora's box by getting involved with the "System," and that our son would suffer for it. I was torn. Of course, I resented being scrutinized and humiliated. It was terrible to realize how I might have contributed to my son's fragile psyche. His father was justified in being suspicious of a system that dehumanized us, painted in broad brush strokes when it came to our son, and applied black and white solutions to such a grey situation. We were frightened, and handling things the best we could, but we had no way of knowing there would be so much more to come.

At fifteen years old, Steven was accused of aggravated indecent liberties with a child after an encounter with a girl two weeks shy of her thirteenth birthday. I feared what my teenage son could not comprehend—his life would never be the same. We had reached a tipping point. After a year of court dates, programs, drug tests, and counseling, Steven was facing next-level consequences. With a lengthy list of infractions and now a potential felony six juvenile conviction (the highest felony level), Steven was likely to be placed into state custody indefinitely. I was shattered. Residential treatment was becoming the most promising option for my son, but that was financially impossible, and I realized I had no alternative but to stand by and watch this surreal drama unfold.

When Steven was first diagnosed with bipolar disorder, I read everything I could about his condition. I was sure I would find an answer—a course of action, some treatment that would set things right. Instead, I was faced with overwhelming hopelessness. After reading one woman's account, I was despondent for days. Life ahead, if it was anything like what these individuals were describing, would be unthinkable. I refused to believe that this was going to be our reality. Even as one of our favorite psychologists explained that Steven would never live a "normal" life on his own—that he would likely require a group home setting at best, and institutionalization at worst—I simply could not accept her prognosis.

What was even more traumatizing were statistics about bipolar disorder and suicide. According to several sources, chances were that my son would end his life in a haze of loneliness and depression, or as a result of some manic, impulsive decision. I was terrified that a tragic end was likely, but I was fighting the tide. Then there were long-term psychological effects on the rest of our family to consider, how our lives would be forever altered. My dreams for my family became a series of nightmares.

I was convinced Steven was the victim of some horrible miscarriage of justice when he was accused of that felony six crime after an afternoon at the park with a couple of kids from the neighborhood. Later he told me some kind of sexual experimentation was going on between the three of them, but the girl "changed her mind." The stories they told never quite added up, but Steven maintained his innocence.

There were many conflicting accounts of what occurred that day, but I had to be the one who listened to my son. I needed to believe him and to be his advocate. Still, I was not blind to the fact that I had given Steven the benefit of the doubt all too often in the past, and it was possible he was not telling the truth. Regardless, I tried to support him. In his case, it did not matter—I could only be a spectator in this bizarre drama, and I was unsure which was worse—standing by as my son was harshly punished for something he did not do, or accepting he was guilty. Either way, my fear and grief were unbearable.

Steven spent several weeks in the Juvenile Detention Center "JDC," or "juvie," as it was known by kids his age. Eventually, my son was sent to a transitional facility while awaiting his court date. Eventually, he was convicted of the felony six offense. Even more shocking, he was given adult-level consequences, because of our county's no-tolerance policy. My darkest fears were realized when his picture and personal information were posted online. Scrolling through images of criminals in the state database—grown men who were convicted abusers, pedophiles, and rapists—there was the adolescent face of my fifteen-year-old son, now a registered sex offender.

Steven was court ordered to a residential facility. I visited regularly, usually bringing snacks and sometimes meals when allowed. He attended school on the premises and did well in his classes, participated in chapel, and impressed his teachers with his creativity. Over time, he completed the program, having met all the court mandated requirements. When he was released, his father insisted that he leave the state, and Steven naturally wanted the opportunity to reunite with his brothers. So, he moved in with his dad almost one thousand miles away, leaving the wreckage of the past four years behind.

For a time, I thought we might cheat fate, but that was wishful thinking. The "Steven years," (before, during, and right after puberty) were chaotic. But between the ages of 18 and 20, there was a brief respite when he was active in a church. He found purpose in Evangelical Christianity and thrived in a regimen of Bible studies, community activities, Sunday services, and a full-time job. During this time, he was able to not only obtain his GED, but he contacted an attorney and went through a process by which his juvenile record was expunged. He was so proud that he was working nights at a manufacturing plant, and even more proud that he was taking control of his life. In those days, Steven called regularly, updating me about the progress his attorney was making on his case. I was supportive, never telling him what I knew to be true— even though his record might be "expunged," he would never be able to remove his image and information from the online sex offender registry. The internet was unforgiving.

During his weekly updates, he told me stories about work and explored enrolling in community college. He spent most of his free time practicing his guitar, writing songs, and volunteering at church. I recognized a familiar pattern; even though Steven resisted it, structure helped him flourish. When he was in "juvie" he read several books and his grades improved for the first time since grade school. In state custody, he thrived in the kind of routine that only an institution with staff can provide. While living on his own, having a set of strict Biblical standards afforded him a moral compass and the kind of regimen that allowed him to function well—for a time.

Steven was militant in his Christianity, and he had a tendency to badger everyone around him with his born-again rhetoric. But he seemed happy and healthy, and that was all that mattered to me. He led a Bible study group for troubled young men at the church and found a supportive community there. I was hopeful that he might be able to settle into his life. Maybe the worst was behind us. After all, when grounded and focused, Steven was a force of nature and showed himself to be a charismatic leader. Things were looking up.

Peaceful times, however, were always exceptions to the rule. Unfortunately, a crisis of faith caused Steven to sever his relationship with his church family. He was devastated when he called to tell me how disillusioned he had become with the leaders, and he realized religion was a charade. My heart broke. I knew this unfortunate shift would disrupt all the progress he had made. Still, there was nothing I could do to help my son as he began to spiral. Steven became unmoored. Within a week he quit his job, sold or gave away all his belongings, and set out in a car he had recently purchased on eBay—a white convertible Toyota Celica.

For a short while he stayed with Travis, who was now married and living in a small Midwestern town. That didn't last; but Steven's talent, tenacity, and charm were his saving grace. This was clear when as a self-taught guitarist, he became a full-time music instructor at a local music store at twenty-one years old. He moved in with his grandmother while teaching guitar nearby. Although it appeared things were improving, I was accustomed to the cycle, and held my breath as I waited for the signs, cracks in the facade so-to-speak that would signal the wild ride was beginning again.

Not long after, Steven became excited about some new herbal substitute for marijuana that he said was "legal." He found a local store where he could buy "K2," also known as "bath salts" or "spice." I tried to press him for more information, but he was euphorically vague. Soon, his father called to tell me what he had been reading about the dangerous synthetic drug. It was too late. Steven dysregulated rapidly. He completely disassembled his Celica in my mother's garage, walked away from his job at the music store because he could hear people's thoughts, and left his grandmother's car running at the curb of the local municipal airport while he boarded a one-way flight back to his dad's. When he finally called, I begged him to check into the hospital after he told me that birds were speaking to him. Instead, he convinced his father to buy him a bus ticket and headed West, living on the streets and under bridges, busking his way from Oregon to California and back again.

For long stretches, Steven would be out of contact. When he reemerged, he would ask for a copy of his birth certificate (so he could apply for a replacement ID), another cell phone, or a cheap guitar since the last one had been stolen or lost. I would be relieved to find out he was in jail or the hospital, because the alternative was perpetual anxiety, insomnia, and a deep physical ache in the center of my chest that made everyday tasks seem dreadful. Knowing Steven's whereabouts brought peace of mind only briefly, because time had shown that he was not likely to get the treatment he needed. He would be discharged and back on the street in a matter of hours, or at most, a few days. The hard truth was, no one had any idea how to help my son. There were stopgap measures, best guesses, and "band-aids," but effective solutions seemed out of reach. Adding to this frustration, Steven did not believe he needed help; he was on some grand adventure. When bad things happened, he just moved on with an uncanny ability to land on his feet. He would find his way to a hospital or community-based services. At the very least, he had learned to advocate for himself.

As I relived the past during my days in Hawai'i, I tried to remember that Steven's situation was not about me. But it was far too easy to calculate all of the reasons why his arc from precocious boy, to bipolar adolescent, to adult transient was my fault. I had my children when I was too young. Their father and I both came from dysfunctional families. We were divorced. We disciplined them too much; they weren't disciplined enough. And in the end, I could not protect them from the world or from each other.

The month I was in Hawai'i, Steven was about to turn thirty. By law, he was "in charge" of his life, but that had led to his hospitalization, and now the courts were making his decisions for him. His father and I had often discussed whether our adult son was capable of managing on his own. We researched options, and whether any of them were actually feasible. We each tried to intervene on Steven's behalf at various times. He lived with several family members over the years, and each time a cycle of hope would begin. The pattern was: temporary stability, a slow deterioration, and finally, a reluctant recognition of the downward spiral. Those of us who love Steven have had no choice but to accept the cycles of helplessness, frustration, and sorrow. It has become evident that we do not possess the knowledge, emotional stamina, or financial resources to help him; good intentions and love are not enough.

My son's elaborate journey initiated personal journeys for those who love him. His brothers struggle with their feelings about the emotional trauma they endured; I know they must be conflicted about how much they love their brother, and how much they resent him. I understand how agonizing those feelings can be. Although my divorce from Steven's father was painful, there have been times when we have called on one another for support as we process our bewilderment, anger, and grief. In those moments, we recognize that no one can empathize the way we can for one another. It is because of Steven that we have evolved, set aside our differences, and mellowed over the years. At least now, we can be kind to each other. Steven has left an undeniable mark on all of us.

Like so many parents, I owe much of my personal growth and emotional development to my relationships with my children; more specifically, the process of learning to love them without expectations. When I left for the island in May of 2018, I had been working with my meditation teacher Thom for over six years. Our work taught me to integrate my grief into daily life, to make space for it, and to respect rather than repress it. I was no longer unconsciously governed by grief or guilt, and part of my evolution was an intentional reframing of my experience, balancing my role as mother with the rest of my identity. For years, I introduced myself as "Steven's mother," "Travis's mother," or "Devin's mother." It took many more years to establish an identity that included motherhood as a part but not the whole of my existence. Had I continued to over-identify with my role as "mother" over the next decade, I fear I would have been lost in martyrdom and regret.

I am no longer defined by my role as mother, but I do not reject mothering. However, there was a time when I insisted that I was not a mother—that I no longer wanted to be responsible for "mothering." That denial was born from grief rather than an abandonment of motherhood. My sons were adults. They did not require the same kind of mothering they once did; in fact they rejected it. Motherhood in many ways was traumatic throughout Steven's youth. Add to that having to accept the absence of my oldest and youngest sons in order to protect them from my middle child, and it's easy to understand how for many years, grief was the engine that drove every aspect of my life.

Once my sons had grown, and my role as mother shifted, I floundered. In response to my claims at the time that I was no longer a mother, my teacher would simply stare at me: "You'll *always* be a mother," he said. I knew he was right, but I had to reconfigure what that meant, especially since Steven monopolized so much of my emotional capacity, worrying where he was and what would happen next. Ironically, it was the complicated nature of my relationship with my son and the bittersweet pain of loving him unconditionally that taught me how to mother in healthy ways.

Although my bond with Steven was a key to my personal growth, I was mystified by the chasm between us during my visits to the hospital. It was as if he was in a different dimension. In his world, he saw and heard things I could not, and there was little I could do but love him from a distance. Sitting across from my son, only a three-foot table between us, proximity was the new challenge. I had to adapt and realign in every moment in order to keep from being swept away in a sea of emotion. I called Thom. With five thousand miles of ocean between us, he reminded me that love did not mean holding on, it meant letting go.

No matter how uncomfortable, exhausted, or sad I felt, I was determined to show up at the hospital bearing my offerings of fast food and candy. After all, it was my duty as Steven's mother. He would have a feral look about him at times, but I caught glimpses of the beautiful boy I remembered. Still, communicating with him was like trying to have a conversation across a massive, turbulent sea. Once in a while, after long periods of silence, he would say something that reminded me of all the late night conversations we had years before—questions like: "Mom, what do you think about time travel?" "Do you believe in God?" "Do you think magic is real?"

It was Steven who would be the first to validate the person I was becoming years before, when I began taking my first college courses. During those golden years (when he was focused and lucid), he encouraged me to explore an identity beyond motherhood. He was not only curious about me and what I was thinking, he challenged me to break out of negative patterns that held me back from experiencing a more fulfilled life. We were friends, and I missed him. In a brief moment of clarity that June, he acknowledged all I had accomplished since I had last seen him six years prior, making a point to congratulate me on completing my PhD, and my career as a professor. He was impressed by the grant I received that allowed me to come to Hawai'i. Yet, I had to wonder if he truly understood the role he played, and how much I had grown because of him. The reality is that without my son's support years before, as well as all of the challenges he forced me to face, I am not sure if I would have been in a position to meet him there on the island in 2018.

Over the past twenty years, there have been many times I nearly gave up. Any parent or person who loves someone with a mental illness knows the despair that comes without warning. So, it was humbling when my son talked about gratitude. He told me several times that he was glad to be alive, and fortunate to be in the hospital where he was safe. In those moments, my personal suffering was put in check—it seemed insignificant and out of place. Here was this insightful but troubled young man, living with the interminable noise of schizophrenia, expressing gratitude to be institutionalized, talking about his desire to help others and share whatever he had with whomever he could. It was unreal, and I was simultaneously shattered by grief and bursting with joy. My adult life has been all about learning and living this paradox, and it all hinges on one thing—being *with* the pain, without anesthetizing, denying, or resisting it.

My journey with Steven has been an initiation. Now, as I survey the pieces of this emotional puzzle, I relive that moment: sitting with my son in a psychiatric ward on an island in the middle of the North Pacific Ocean. Years of powerlessness, rage, and grief brought me to a place of acceptance. However, in my experience, acceptance is not something attained; neither is it a final destination. It is an evolution. The wheel spins—sometimes slowly, sometimes rapidly—each emotional turn is intense but familiar, seemingly eternal, yet temporary. My son's schizoaffective disorder, with its highs and lows, otherworldly insights, and mysterious cycles paradoxically holds the key. It teaches those of us who love him to reflect, not only upon our experiences with him, but on our own trauma and the potential treasure awaiting us. He teaches us what it is to be broken, to despair, and to confront our demons. He models resilience and calls it forth in each of us. It is because of Steven that we are driven to that most agonizing yet rewarding point of vulnerability, where raw honesty and surrender show us what it means to love unconditionally.

CHAPTER THREE

Re-Storied

Myths and stories have an uncanny way of making meaning out of memories. They also provide a way to process grief and access the wisdom needed to survive despair. In sharing my memories, as well as the myths and stories that continue to speak to my own Mother/s Odyssey, my hope is that others might find them helpful as they undergo their grief passages. Memories, like stories, can be elusive, and they are prone to interpretation. My story at times conflicts with those of my sons. This is because stories carry ambiguity, and memories illustrate a similar fluidity. They take on a life of their own, providing a particular insight at a given time. I cannot say that my memories of these events are exactly the way things were, though they are based on my experiences. This is simply a story to place alongside so many other stories of grief. In so doing, one discovers the potential for transformation.

The beauty of stories is that they have the power to reassemble the pieces of fractured hopes and expectations, like broken pottery repaired with liquid precious metals in the Japanese art of *kintsugi*. With *kintsugi*, what is fragmented is restored (or rather *re-storied*); the scars tell a redemption tale. Embellished with gold and silver, they generate a new kind of beauty and wholeness. My story, as it is written here, is part of a mythological project, which gathers stories together, arranges and looks closely at them in an effort to extract meaning. It is my way of applying gold to the fractured pieces of my broken heart; myths and stories facilitate that restoration.

Such stories are found in a number of places: in myths and sacred texts, in folktales and fiction. They live in cherished recollections, well-guarded secrets, and in quiet conversations over coffee. Wherever they are found, they burn brighter when in the company of other redemption stories. Their irresistible allure draws us closer, especially when we find common ground or a particular resonance that captures the imagination. Stories preserve information and divine wisdom; as we visit them time and again, what we need (or rather, what we are ready to receive) is there for us, ever-evolving—taking us a little deeper with each retelling. This was the hope I was seeking.

Toni Morrison's *Beloved* is one story that came to represent healing for me. Her novel is a depiction of living grief—not only a mother's grief, but the collective grief of a people wounded by the brutality and injustice of slavery. She exposes the specter of the dark mother, causing her readers to wrestle with redemption, madness, and the mystical aspects of memory. Her narrative traverses a bridge from trauma to transformation, providing context for personal and collective grief. It gives us a *living* story and a way to talk about emotions that are almost too much to bear.

Beloved opened my eyes to the power of story-making, and the capacity for stories to promote individual and communal healing. Morrison drags living grief out into the light of day for all to see. Her protagonist, Sethe, is the embodiment of trauma and grief. She is the dark mother; the one who poses the question whether death would be better than living in bondage. Moreover, the dark mother is the one who is willing to answer that question without hesitation. When Sethe murders her young daughter in order to save her from the torture and bondage of slavery, she exemplifies the ferocity and decisiveness of the dark mother. As a psychic metaphor, she demonstrates a force that brings about the end of things. When the threat presses in, and we find ourselves needing to take action—especially action that causes tremendous inner conflict—drawing upon the dark mother can direct energy and focus toward what must be done.

Beloved also demonstrates how healing manifests when trauma and grief (and the dark mother) are acknowledged. Healing comes when we give voice to grief, and when we bear witness to the stories of others. In Morrison's work, this is evident when Paul D (Sethe's companion), having survived torture and humiliation at the hands of slave masters, wants to "put his story next to hers." Sethe's trauma allows her to acknowledge Paul D's pain even before he can—since he sealed it up in a "tin box" where his "red heart" once resided—whereas Paul D's empathy is born out of agony and shame. As a result, he is able to bear witness to Sethe's grief by acknowledging what she cannot. Further, in witnessing her pain and her darkness, and accepting her in spite of it,

Paul D shows Sethe how she can begin to forgive herself.

In her grief over her dead child (and in confronting the horror of what she has done), Sethe is despondent, taken to her bed, awaiting death. Once the ghost of her murdered child is put to rest, she laments that Beloved—her "best thing"—has left her. Paul D counters with the famous line: "You your own best thing, Sethe. You are." At her bedside, Paul D sees (bears witness to) the "good" mother *and* the murderous mother. Through this act of witnessing, and by laying his story alongside Sethe's, Morisson ends her novel with a promise of healing and redemption for even the darkest of mothers.

My Mother/s Odyssey resonated with the deep chord Morrison struck in *Beloved*: the necessity of the dark mother, and the realization that healing and redemption emerge out of story-making. Writing this book has been a process of disentangling my personal story from Steven's. Like Sethe, I had to come to terms (for better or worse) with the good mother, as well as the dark mother aspects of myself. Before I could reimagine an identity uncoupled from my role as the grieving mother, I had to face and begin the work of integrating *all* aspects of mothering in myself. Morrison's *Beloved* artfully modeled how stories are a catalyst for this inner work.

In searching for stories to set alongside my own, I found they came through strangers, acquaintances, or friends. Sometimes, they came from myths, legends, and folktales. The power of stories is in their ability to bring definition (and re-definition) to the experiences that make up our lives. We long for stories—we invent them, we piece them back together from remnants and fragmented memories. We are compelled to tell them, to hear them, and to commit them to memory. Why? In my case, because I learned from stories how to heal, how to restore, and how to return from a Mother/s Odyssey transformed. My friend and colleague, Dr. Jaffa Vernon Frank,[*] explains it best:

> When facing life's most challenging aspects—illness, loss, alienation, physical or psychological pain, death—the stories we embrace are instrumental to our restoration. The capacity to engage the experiencing body, creative imagination, and

---

[*] Jaffa Vernon Frank is one of three real names I use in this book (alongside Dennis Patrick Slattery and Thom) because I cite her work *Eyes of the Gorgon*. The rest have been changed.

narrating mind in a healing collaboration in response to pain and loss is a form of grace; a mystery that transforms the experience of hardship without denying the truth of suffering.[3]

Jaffa's experience with living grief gave her the ability to stay with me on the phone moments after I discovered my son had left the continent during his manic episode in April, 2013. Her story was the one that came to mind during my emotional meltdown in a strip mall parking lot. Intuitively, I knew she could enter that dark place with me. When my friend speaks of "grace," she knows it in her flesh and bones, through her "experiencing body." As a result, she held fast with compassionate acceptance as I buckled under waves of anguish, rage, and despair. I felt then what Morrison was conveying in her conclusion to *Beloved*—when at Seth's bedside, Paul D came to lay his story next to hers.

The "healing collaboration" Jaffa described was manifest in her presence. Able to bear witness to my grief, she gestured toward acceptance and transformation without "denying the truth" of my suffering. This denial happens when well-meaning individuals minimize grief by offering platitudes, or simply avoid it altogether. One can hardly blame them since grief can be messy, repulsive, and downright terrifying. Still, as Jaffa suggests, grace (or transformation through loss) is the ultimate gift.

Those who are familiar with living grief recognize it and develop a unique capacity to comfort others. That comfort comes most often through compassionate listening, validating another's experience, and sharing one's stories. Many individuals have shared their stories over the course of my pilgrimage, providing empathy, encouragement, and inspiration. These angels have ministered to me along the way, nurturing and coaxing me back to life. Actually, they were not angels at all—they were not from another realm, but emerged out of the very depths of grief in which I found myself.

Stories reveal that this kind of listening, acknowledging, and nurturing is what leads to restoration (or restory-ing). A particularly relevant example is the ancient myth of Inanna, Queen of Heaven. This Sumerian myth is considered one of the oldest in recorded history. Many stories which come after reflect its themes. Inanna (also known as Ishtar) wished to enter the Underworld to attend the funeral of her brother-in-law. Her sister Ereshkigal was less than happy about her arrival, since she was convinced that Inanna's hidden motives were to expand her own kingdom, not to properly grieve her husband. Inanna, who was ushered through seven gates to reach her sister's throne, was stripped of her jewelry and clothing as she passed each threshold. Finally, brought before Ereshkigal naked and properly humbled, her sister issued her death sentence.

Upon her death, Inanna's corpse was suspended on a hook in the Underworld. Cleverly, she thought to prepare for her incapacitation, instructing her handmaid to call on the gods if she did not return in three days. One of the gods (Enki), finally responded, creating two small creatures which he dispatched to bring Inanna the food and water of life. In addition, Enki charged them to empathize with Ereshkigal's outrage and despair. Moved by their compassion, the Queen of the Underworld granted them a request. They asked for Inanna's corpse, which was reconstituted by the divine nourishment those two small creatures carried into the Underworld.

When I discovered my son had taken a one-way flight to Honolulu and within a week I lost contact with him, I felt like Inanna hanging on that hook. Everything had been stripped away, and I was condemned to death, a lifeless corpse. Even today, the brutal and abject annihilation of Inanna's descent into the Underworld resonates with the human experience of living grief. Her ordeal is an illustration of the Mother/s Odyssey, the grief passage where suffering, surrender, and death are natural and necessary. Furthermore, Enki's emissaries are an illustration of how compassion heals: by descending into the treacherous realm of grief, and carrying out their master's orders to listen, empathize, and nourish, they activated Inanna's healing and restoration. However, the Queen of Heaven was resurrected only after the two divine emissaries ministered to her sister. They offered the compassion and empathy Ereshkigal needed in order to transform her rage into reason. Then, they could turn their attention to Inanna.

For me, Jaffa was like those divine emissaries, able to listen without judgment or attachment, empathizing with my travail, nurturing me back to reason. I was not left hanging on that hook alone with all of the life drained out of me like Inanna. Nor was I left to labor in agony like Ereshkigal. When I pulled into the parking lot that day, I was paralyzed— enraged that my son had slipped through the cracks once again. The very supports that were in place to keep him from acting impulsively had failed. It had been several months since I laid eyes on him, and now the separation became even more severe. Overwhelmed by despair, I could not imagine going about my day, driving my car, grading papers, or even continuing to breathe. My friend was present to my heartbreak with an ability to know the emotions I was experiencing. She carried with her divine gifts: the food and water of life. And I was able to cycle through another turn in the grief passage. I could, indeed, continue.

When applying a mythological lens to the story of Inanna, it becomes evident that grief is a natural cycle; and these cycles of descent and return are recurring. The nonnegotiable price of the grief passage is the loss of everything one holds dear. I had lost my ability to influence my son's path, to intervene when things went wrong. These, of course, were matters out of my control. They always had been, but I had been in denial. It was my denial, my desire to control, and a dream-version of Steven's life which was dangling from that unforgiving meat-hook.

The myth of Inanna confirms that grief, while annihilating, is nonetheless transformative. In the end, acknowledgement and forgiveness herald regeneration. Furthermore, just as Inanna is stripped and condemned to death, the Mother/s Odyssey requires that we must die to some part of ourselves. Some might argue that it is the ego that must die, but the ego is something with which one must always contend.[4] And so, we will cycle again and again, letting go of our attachments to the way things are "supposed" to be, surrendering to the unknown, and dying to our idealized versions of ourselves and those we love. There is comfort in knowing that living grief "mythically" means setting it alongside the grief of others, paying attention to the themes and symbols in the stories, and experiencing resonance where it may be found.

The Greek myth of Demeter and Persephone is another tale of a Mother/s Odyssey.[5] Demeter, the Divine Mother, endured profound grief when her daughter, Persephone, was abducted by Hades and taken to the Underworld where he resided as King. In the prime of life, the young maiden was coerced into marrying him after eating three pomegranate seeds, and there she remained as his Queen for eternity. Persephone was warned that consuming anything while she was in Hades would prevent her from leaving, but she could not resist.

Once her mother discovered Persephone was missing, she was out of her mind. Demeter exhausted herself searching for her missing daughter. When she found that her brother Zeus gave Hades his blessing to carry out this diabolical plan, the Mother of the Harvest became so enraged that she cursed the land, refusing to allow any crops to flourish.

Indeed, the volatile emotions of her living grief eradicated all potential nourishment and growth. This story echoes the myth of Inanna in the intensity of Demeter's emotion, the Underworld reference, and the cycles of descent and return.

Confounded by Demeter's rage, the gods intervene to preserve cosmic order. Similar to the negotiation between Ereshkigal and Inanna, they facilitate an arrangement whereby Persephone would remain in the Underworld for half of the year, returning to her mother for the other half. Demeter's living grief, reactivated every time her daughter descended to Hades, is reflected in the "death" that fall and winter represent. Likewise, upon Persephone's return, Demeter's relief is symbolized by the emergence of spring, as well as the abundance of the late summer harvest.

While the Greek myth of Demeter and Persephone is certainly a mythological way to understand the seasons, it is also a vivid reading of living grief, where one finds themselves in a continual pattern of separation and reunion. I found myself entering and exiting these seasons each time Steven resurfaced from his long mysterious absences, both physical and psychological, and each time he was lured by the call of the Underworld forces. Then, I felt the helplessness, sorrow, and rage all over again. In my experience, loving someone with schizophrenia replicates that pattern, and it is something I am continually learning to accept.

Even though she was the Mother Goddess, Demeter was unable to alter the course of her daughter's fate. Filled with rage, helplessness, and despair—emotions intrinsic to the Mother/s Odyssey—she too had to accept the outcome and make peace with the other gods, which entailed forgiving them. Perhaps she also had to forgive Persephone for her naiveté, for foolishly eating the pomegranate seeds, and for falling for Hades and maturing into her role as Queen. Certainly, Demeter had to forgive herself for being unable to prevent her daughter's abduction in the first place. This part of the story reflected my ambivalence about my son's choice to leave the mainland, my rage at a system that continued to fail him, and my own guilt for not keeping careful enough watch.

The Demeter myth also illustrated that the ebbs and flows of living grief were like the tide; they were cyclical like the seasons. Moreover, the resilience of the mother/daughter relationship between Demeter and Persephone was a tribute to the transformative process of separation, loss, and restoration. Whichever point I was experiencing on my grief passage was temporary; but that meant my physical connection to and separation from my son was also temporary. Even so, I felt that eternal resilience, and mythological stories of the Underworld descent became a ray of light—there was meaning in the madness.

In the early 90s, Clarissa Pinkola Estes' work was my first exposure to a mythological approach. She provided a delightful interpretation of Demeter's story in *Women Who Run with the Wolves*, emphasizing irreverence and bawdy humor as the tonic for Demeter's grief. She pointed to the kinds of conversations between friends when no one is listening—the way women talk late at night in the company of other women (and plenty of wine). The obscenity and dark humor Estés spoke of is reminiscent of ancient goddess cults, and it is embodied by Baubo, the earthy crone goddess who lifts her skirt and cracks wise using her vulva as her mouth, making Demeter laugh in spite of herself. This crude irreverence is at times characterized by the crone; it is what breaks the spell of grief in this case. The crone wisdom Estés explores in her book is unapologetically risqué, infused with black humor, and brutally honest. It is a necessary and welcome instigator, and a key ingredient to renewal.

Crone wisdom emanates from those who have suffered. They have seen it all, having passed through their own descent and return, likely more than once. Crone wisdom not only "knows," it is the very manifestation of the transformation the grief passage demands. Baubo is able to disarm the stifling grief that threatens to destroy the living by telling dirty jokes and salacious stories; she causes Demeter to laugh unselfconsciously. The crone is not intimidated by rage, agony, or annihilation. She embraces all, casting a mischievous wink at the good mother and the dark mother alike. Her cackle is infectious. It generates healing, a shift in perspective, and signals that life goes on.

I too would encounter the crone. She showed up in myths and stories, but also through friends and mentors, men and women who grieved all manner of losses. They were my divine emissaries; they listened with compassion, validated my emotions, and nurtured me back to life. They made me laugh in spite of my sorrow, and helped me to recognize that it was possible to make sense of the senselessness of living grief. They helped me find a new narrative by telling me their stories— and I began to "re-story" the tragedy of my son's illness, as well as my own heartbreak.

CHAPTER FOUR

Our Lady of Sorrows

I don't hide my grief from people in my day-to-day life, but I don't advertise it either. My grief passage, or Mother/s Odyssey so to speak, has been a guiding force. Learning how to love someone with a diagnosis like schizophrenia is a process, and I continue to develop a better understanding as my relationship with Steven evolves. When he was a teenager, we talked about writing a book together. We wanted to explore what we were learning about mental illness. At that time, he was too young to understand the implications of consent. I worried he might later regret a decision about going public with his diagnosis. At nineteen, he encouraged my writing and sometimes sent me his own projects. I was unsure about my ability to tell this story, and I was concerned about how family members might feel. I reasoned that waiting would resolve any misgivings I had.

Yet another decade had passed, Steven was in his thirties, and I was even more uncertain than ever as to whether he could give consent or make rational decisions. Despite his mental illness (or rather, because of it), my son was an extraordinary friend. His love and encouragement sustained me through many trying times. But now, his spirit—the essence that was so vibrantly "Steven" for as long as I could remember—seemed far removed. In sharing how our relationship endures, and how Steven's influence changed my life, I hope to keep our connection alive. I have learned to be clear about the distinction between my son's experience and my own, in order to give him the dignity and respect he deserves. This is not "our" story—it cannot be. It would be wrong to try to tell Steven's story; I can only tell my own. Oddly, the telling of it somehow allows me to feel close to him and to bear the heartache not only of the loss of my son, but the absence of my very special friend.

It has not been easy to disentangle our stories. For years, it felt like my entire world was consumed by Steven. I was susceptible to bouts of depression, especially during the years when he was off the grid. How could I have known how prophetic it was to call him my "transient sleeper" when he was just a boy? I cannot calculate the hours I spent worrying that he was lost, alone and afraid, or the sleepless nights on the internet trying to find any trace of him in the news, in public records, or in published obituaries across the country. Once, his mug shot appeared in an Oregon database, and my son's vacant eyes shot like a spear straight through my heart. Still, I kept that picture close. It was all I had. Then, there was the time he called from a hospital, where he had been admitted after being beaten and dropped off at a 7-11 while hitchhiking to Los Angeles. I scrambled to find a way to get to him, but within twenty-four hours he was released, and I lost contact again.

My imagination often led me to believe that Steven was living a life of loneliness. Ironically, during my stay in Hawai'i, it did not take long to see that he was anything but lonely. He was so preoccupied by ongoing conversations with the "others" that I had to wonder if he ever experienced stillness, let alone loneliness. Occasionally, Steven expressed a desire for a relationship, saying he would like to find a girlfriend, but he rarely mentioned loneliness. I began to suspect that it was my loneliness from missing and worrying about him that caused me to believe he felt like I did.

Even though relationships mattered to him, they were not as much of a concern for my son as they were for me. I shuddered to think of Steven as a vagrant, living a solitary life. And yet, during our conversations while I was in Hawai'i, he reminisced about his life on the street, speaking of it with a mixture of nostalgia and pride. Even as he recounted dangerous moments, by and large his lifestyle seemed to suit his wanderlust. The constant flow of thoughts and images comprising his mental landscape coincided with his transient nature. I saw that our ways of seeing the world were vastly different.

All of the suffering I created, imagining scenarios that "might" be playing out in Steven's life, was wasted energy. The truth was that no amount of catastrophizing, obsessing, or holding vigil ever made a difference. Many times, I worked myself into a panic, which accomplished nothing, and left me exhausted and emotionally bankrupt. I learned to manage the extreme emotions associated with my living grief by recognizing their futility.

If my anguish had any measurable impact, I would have willingly carried it forever. Most parents know the irresistible impulse to do whatever it takes to prevent their child's pain. Equally as many come to realize that they can only offer love and support while their adult children live their lives, make their mistakes, and bear their own burdens. Knowing when to step in and when to step back is a precarious dance. Even though I recognize that the traumas and tragedies of my life made me who I am today, I find myself compelled to rob my sons of those same opportunities.

With this in mind, I was drawn to the image of Mary, mother of Jesus, knowing she witnessed her son's unjust torture and death. While I did not have an idealized vision of Steven as a savior, like most parents, I was convinced my sons were extraordinary. Instead, I vacillated between two poles—one accepted the divine order in my son's circumstances, our intertwined paths, and how schizoaffective disorder had been an unlikely gift. The other pole was where I found myself all too often, despising the injustice of his illness, and feeling victimized by powerlessness. In the tension between these poles is where transformation was born.

Mary's image was a testament to the transformation brought about by a Mother/s Odyssey. Her deified presence as the Mother of Christ was a symbol of living grief. She reflected the agony of helplessly standing by while a loved one suffered. The death of a child is generally considered one of the most excruciating experiences one can endure, and as the grieving mother, Mary became an icon of tranquility and acceptance.

Compared to the internal violence I felt while grieving, the image of the stoic and deferential Mary seemed ludicrous. For me, it was an affront. Even though I was at first offended by her composure, I found myself coming back again and again to marvel at her serenity. She had something I craved: peace of mind. In the face of her son's agony, she did not waver—she did not intervene. She quietly held vigil throughout his traumatic ordeal. The power in this image was compelling; it was drawing me toward a mythological understanding of my own grief.

It took years for me to see the synchronicity between Steven urging me along my path into religious and mythological studies, and the tools it gave me to heal from his absence. He had been so proud of me for taking my first community college course (World Religions) in 2001, and I wanted to prove to him I could do it; if I could reinvent myself, so could he. But this was new territory, and I was terrified. Steven's enthusiasm motivated me to press on through my fear. Unknowingly, two decades before, my son helped prepare the ground for the healing work I would need to do in order to overcome the most agonizing sorrow I could imagine.

There is a compelling image of Mary with seven swords or daggers embedded in her heart known as "Our Lady of Sorrows" (also "The Softener of Evil Hearts"). Occasionally, depictions of Our Lady of Sorrows display a pained expression, but more often than not she maintains resigned sadness or serene passivity. That same expression can be found on one of the most recognizable Marion icons, Michelango's *Pietà*, housed in Vatican City. Michelangelo's statue depicts the beautiful young Mary cradling the corpse of Jesus on her lap; her face is eerily emotionless. To my mind, it was unlikely that grief could elicit serenity, but Mary's willing acceptance was a clue. It became the key to understanding my living grief.

Our Lady of Sorrows embodies the wounds of a Mother/s Odyssey, evidenced by the seven swords protruding from her chest. Those who experience the anguish of the grief passage know sometimes these wounds are felt as minute cuts, barely noticeable; others weep over time, never healing; and still others cut to the bone, draining one's vital energy. Our Lady speaks to these wounds; however, her passivity is a puzzle. Grief is a more vicious experience than what is portrayed by many of the sanitized versions of Mary I began to investigate. Relative silence in sacred texts regarding grieving mothers simply does not ring true. Anyone who has lost a child, or who has experienced a traumatic separation from a loved one, knows the brutality of grief. So, what does Mary's lack of emotion in so many representations indicate? What fuels her otherworldly ability to bear the unbearable? Is she detached and above it all? Does she possess some supernatural capacity to endure the trauma of watching her son's torture and death unfazed? Certainly not. The mythic import of Mary's image came into view the more I studied it, revealing not only a promise of survival, but the capacity of the grieving heart to thrive despite the mortal wounds it bears.

Initiated by her son's personal journey, Mary's quiet transformation was somewhat downplayed. In Western Catholicism and Eastern Orthodox religion, Mary's seven sorrows were a tribute to her evolution from blessed virgin to icon of compassion; they were evidence of what Frederik Holweck called her "spiritual martyrdom."[6] Spiritual martyrdom insinuates that Mary encountered a Mother/s Odyssey, and the "death" of her identity as earthly mother was the sacrifice for her transformation to eternal mother of all humanity.

The term "martyr" was formerly understood as witness or observer.[7] Each sword that Mary bears is representative of a specific grief wound that occurred as she watched her son's path unfold. These wounds were foretold when a prophet informed her she would 1) endure tremendous grief as a mother. Shortly thereafter, 2) Mary was forced into exile with Jesus in order to protect him. Next, a separation between mother and son occurred when 3) Jesus was "lost" and subsequently found teaching in the temple. This separation demonstrates how maturity thins the ties between mother and child. The sword piercing Mary's heart, symbolic of this thinning, suggests that though it is natural, it is nonetheless painful.

Conversely, Mary's fourth sorrow—seeing her son bruised and broken under the weight of his torture device—is wholly unnatural. The fifth sword marks her powerlessness in the face of his crucifixion; the sixth represents the soldier's spear delivering the final death blow. Jesus died and was removed from the cross. And finally, Our Lady of Sorrows prepared the body of her dead child for burial, and the seventh sword takes up permanent residence in her bleeding heart.

These are Mary's ritually recognized grief encounters in Catholic and Greek Orthodox traditions. And to be fair, celebrations for "The Seven Joys of Mary"[8] are also observed to balance her grief, including (in part) the Annunciation, the Nativity, and the Appearance of the Risen Christ.[9] She therefore reminds us that grief is experienced in counterpoint with joy.

However, as I began to identify with Mary's Mother/s Odyssey, I became more curious about the less severe wounds she endured, wounds which were often ignored. For example, Jesus scolded his mother for imploring him to intervene at a wedding when the hosts ran out of wine (John 2: 1-11). Then, he denied his mother altogether while he was teaching and someone reported that his brother and Mary had arrived. According to Matthew 12:48, he remarked, "Who is my mother? Who is my brother?" These "lesser" wounds represent the discomfort that occurs as mothers learn to release their children into the world.

A mythological reading allows Our Lady of Sorrows, pierced through the heart by seven swords, to become a symbol for those who meet their grief wounds, great and small, with grace and resolve. By these wounds Mary is re-storied—her transformation is realized, and she becomes an archetype of virtue, compassion, and healing. As the Blessed Virgin, she symbolizes the hope of each new parent, but also the innocence of each new endeavor. Her exile represents the insecurity and isolation which occurs when one finds themselves in unknown territory. More specifically, it evokes the primal emotions individuals experience when attempting to protect themselves or someone they love. Mary's tolerance of Jesus's independence, his withdrawal from her, and his personal mission models how one must let go in order for maturity to transpire. As the weeping mother at the foot of the cross, she illustrates how we must often accept powerlessness in the face of the unthinkable. And finally, her pervasive presence which extends beyond Catholicism and Greek Orthodoxy signals the eternal aspect of transformation brought on by the Mother/s Odyssey. Mary's passage from innocent girl, to mother, to grieving mother, and on to revered icon, is a pilgrimage of acceptance. While obviously, Jesus is the focal point for Christianity, as the grieving mother, Mary surreptitiously undergoes her own torture, death, and resurrection; this is the Mother/s Odyssey. In the end, mother and son are simultaneously transformed.

I have encountered many grieving mothers and fathers. As often as I find myself in conversations with individuals diagnosed with mental illness, I find myself in chance meetings with parents who have lost a child, or people who have experienced some kind of profound loss. Perhaps there is a magnetic field among the walking wounded. If one pays attention, odds are they will encounter others like themselves. Do the "crosses" we bear contain a subtly detectable frequency—a subsequent resonance pulling us toward one another, where we seek comfort and compassion? One thing seems clear—living grief has a common language.

So, I really should not have been surprised to encounter Sarah during my stay in Hawai'i. She owned the property where I stayed for a week before settling into the university dorm. We developed an immediate connection and kept in contact throughout my stay on the island. Sarah had lost her twenty-four-year-old daughter when she was randomly hit by a car fourteen years earlier. Within two days, there we were, two complete strangers, sharing our grief stories. We were able to speak to each other with deep empathy, and Sarah offered companionship during a time when I was vulnerable and alone. She truly "got it." One might think that our conversations were depressing; they were anything but. We spoke the language of living grief, which was surprisingly irreverent, joyful, and healing. Yes, there were tears, but mostly our conversations were filled with love and laughter. One day she exclaimed, "We talk about some dark shit, but it's not sad! It makes me happy! It's so *real*." Her words stirred up the memory of the crudely honest humor of Baubo, which was the antidote to Demeter's paralyzing despair. Sarah, for me, was like one of those divine emissaries carrying the food and water of life into my Underworld ordeal. She listened, empathized, and nourished my soul with her presence.

On three occasions, Sarah and I met for lunch or coffee after my visits with Steven. Often, I came away from the hospital feeling like a human root canal, as if some part of me had been ripped out and my nerves were exposed. I struggled with anxiety so overwhelming it would manifest physically. An intense pressure would rise in my throat, and I had difficulty catching my breath. After seeing Steven, I would be on the verge of tears. Sometimes, I was so unsteady, I worried I would not be able to navigate the car from the parking lot to the highway without careening off the side of the mountain.

These moments with Sarah allowed me to decompress before returning to my monastic room at the dorm. Our connection reinforced what we had come to understand about living grief: each day held everything you needed—and that is all there was. While my grief was so intense that getting through the next day or week or year seemed impossible, Sarah showed me that it was okay to laugh. One could dream again; and in the end, you live. She also reminded me to "keep it simple"—one breath, one moment, one cup of coffee was enough.

I sat with Sarah following a visit with Steven one Sunday, after he had touched my arm while we were playing UNO, saying: "I really love you, Mom. I'm so glad you're here." I would savor these peaks on the emotional rollercoaster that was my relationship with my son. The highs and lows were just a part of the cycle. Still, I was always startled by the inevitable plunge. I had learned to diffuse the highs and lows by letting go of expectations, once I became aware of them. However, I was easily caught off-guard. Within minutes, he looked at me and said, "Are you sure you're my real mom?" I assured him I was, then asked him if he thought he was my real son. After a long silence, he muttered, "I'm not really sure what to say about that."

Minutes later, as I reeled from this exchange, Steven showed me a list of things he wanted before I left the island: a watch, a book based on a video game, a CD player, and Battleship, a game he was hoping we could play on our next visit. An ant crawled across his open notebook beside a half-eaten order of Arby's curly fries and four ridiculously small, white Styrofoam cups sharing the contents of one can of root beer. I was allowed to bring soda in cans, but the contents had to be immediately transferred into Styrofoam cups; then, the cans were confiscated. I tried to focus on the list scrawled across the top of Steven's notebook, but could not help staring at several lines halfway down the page:

Perfect Cyborg Build Impact Perfect Cyborg Build Impact
Perfect Cyborg Build Impact Perfect Cyborg Build Impact
Perfect Cyborg Build Impact Perfect Cyborg Build Impact
Perfect Cyborg Build Impact Perfect Cyborg Build Impact
Perfect Cyborg Build Impact Perfect Cyborg Build Impact

The charge nurse came to hustle me out of the room since Steven and I had been visiting for over an hour and others were waiting. Unsteadily, I made my way through security, back to my car where it sat overlooking the bay. In shock from reading my son's strangely coded thoughts, I hesitated to drive the rented Ford Focus back down the mountain. Instead, I texted Sarah. "Hey, wanna grab a coffee?" She shot right back. "Sure, it's on me."

Sarah greeted me with a warm hug, her long blonde hair cascading around her shoulders. She was a little older than me, and had grown up on the island. Sarah carried that free and easy Hawai'i vibe, like walking sunshine and lazy days on the beach. The intense tales of her life were interspersed with surfer-talk that made me smile. "Dude! Keep it simple, man!" She was quirky, and I noticed some people did not know how to respond to her buoyant personality. But I saw another side to Sarah. Her sense of freedom was hard-won. She had truly suffered, not only after her daughter's sudden and violent death, but for years, she too battled self-destructive behavior, painful relationships, and bipolar disorder. Yet, here she was, my angel of mercy, greeting me like a long lost sister.

Sarah wanted to meet Steven. "It'll be great! Be sure to tell him everyone calls me 'Auntie'," she crowed. During my last week on the island, I brought her to the hospital as a potential Narcotics Anonymous (NA) sponsor for Steven. As an NA sponsor, she would be allowed to enter the facility. This was not entirely a ruse. Sarah was familiar with 12-step programs since she had spent years in recovery groups during hospitalizations in the past. She was also living well and managing her bipolar disorder without medication. She told me how she had been overly-sedated and addicted to prescription drugs during the "dark years," and that off and on during that time, she had considered suicide. She explained that the meds were designed to keep her from feeling her grief, which could send her into either uncontrolled mania or fatal depression.

However, Sarah had come to a place in her life where she was able to channel her living grief into life force. She was self-aware and open about her experiences. She vigilantly maintained a lifestyle that allowed her to choose sobriety every day. Her beautiful cabin in the mountains was her reason and reward for acknowledging her limitations and putting in place safeguards to stay on track. When I remarked how impressive this was, she reminded me that it had taken fifty-plus years. I desperately grasped onto the hope in her story. Steven's case might be altogether different, but Sarah was an inspiration. She was a lighthouse in a storm, and I loved her for her ability to be real. More than that, I was grateful she wanted to share her wisdom and experience with my son.

We talked about how our meeting might unfold, having no idea whether she would feel comfortable or whether Steven would be receptive. I was concerned this could be awkward or triggering for Sarah, but she was excited about what she considered a "full-circle" event. She had been in and out of hospitals and psychiatric wards since she was twelve, and the hospital where Steven was housed had been her first stop. There was something bigger at work here that was not lost on me.

While she was much more effusive than those blasé depictions of Mary, I saw that Sarah was going through life with her own swords embedded in her heart. The light shining around her was not in spite of them, it was in a sense enhanced by their presence, as if glinting and glimmering off of the gilded, jewel-encrusted hilts of those blades. Sarah was showing me how life could be, how one lived with grief and experienced joy—how to show up, take risks, and embrace what was presented in each moment.

On our way to the hospital, we stopped to pick up root beer and a Hawaiian pizza from Little Caesar's at Steven's request. Then, we passed through all the routine levels of security. I braced for this entire scheme to crumble, afraid some authority figure would intercept our plan. But, we pulled it off, and before long, the three of us were crammed into the awkward visiting room, sitting around a collapsible banquet table which Steven happily assembled. The week before, I told him about Sarah. He was curious, but I was taken by surprise at how quickly they fell into a lively conversation. Sarah was wonderful, listening intently and deciphering Steven's awkward speech. We spent two hours snacking, talking, and playing a hilarious game of UNO.

I was amazed by my son's transformation. He had not been this animated or spoken so coherently in years. With Sarah, he laughed for the first time since I had been visiting—really laughed—teasing us as he one-upped the two of us at cards. He entertained Sarah with stories from his childhood. One of his favorites was about me soaking a neighbor with a garden hose after she threatened three-year-old Steven and his brothers, calling them dirty Mexicans and screaming at us to "Go back to Mexico!" I glanced at my new friend sheepishly. Somehow, her presence allowed my son to connect with his life in a way I could not. He was present.

As Steven became more comfortable, he talked about his "voices" and the struggles of being homeless. I observed the two of them: my son, more alive than I had seen him over the past thirty days, and Sarah's magical demeanor, easy and fun. They made plans to connect in the weeks ahead. Steven suggested buying an NA workbook and offered to requisition money from his payee to cover Sarah's gas if she would be willing to come back and work on it with him. She was gracious and encouraging, which seemed to enliven his intelligence and humor.

As we pulled away from the hospital, my new friend looked at me, her gaze relaxed and reassuring. She said the situation was not as bad as I feared in the psych ward, explaining that she had seen a lot worse. She was impressed by Steven's wit and generosity, commenting on how special he was while acknowledging he had some significant challenges. Although I felt strangely detached, Sarah was optimistic and peaceful about his prospects, and I wondered if I dared to dream once again of a life free from schizoaffective disorder for my son. Would Steven be able to find his place in the world, a little piece of paradise on the side of a mountain? Would I?

As I drove, Sarah stared out the window at the mountain range; embodying that serene look on Mary's face, she was my patron saint of survival. She had endured, and like Our Lady of Sorrows she had become an ambassador to the broken-hearted. Something shifted in what felt like the frozen sea of my emotions. Like melting ice floes, I sensed a breaking away—an all but imperceptible glide toward hope. I wanted to believe that my pain would subside, but how could I withstand   another disappointment? Reluctantly, I let myself exhale, and my heart stirred. With all that Sarah had gone through to get to this moment, with all of the agony her mother's heart had endured, here she was calmly encouraging me. Since there was not a disingenuous bone in her body, I took solace in the connection that formed that evening, knowing that my time on the island was coming to an end.

CHAPTER FIVE

Call Me Crazy

When someone is diagnosed with a mental illness, it is not uncommon for family members to question their own sanity. I certainly have. Many individuals living with severe mental health challenges have extraordinary talents and abilities. For this reason, I am uncomfortable with the term "illness." Unfortunately, it is commonplace to describe those who experience the world differently by applying pathological terms like "illness" or "disorder." However, the reality is much more complex.

Loving a person with these labels can make one "crazy." Their unique presence can be both irresistible and infuriating, and maintaining a stable relationship can be a struggle. With keen intuition, sensitivity, and awe-inspiring creative energy, they are often clever and quite charismatic. These unique souls sometimes exude spiritual knowledge and otherworldly insights like those of prophets or healers. Like shamans, medicine men and women, and gurus of various practices (whose "gifts" read like a page out of *The Diagnostic and Statistical Manual of Mental Disorders,* the Bible of psychological diagnoses), it sometimes feels as if these individuals can see right through us. Most "holy" people or saints of old, would be considered mentally "ill" by Western standards. In fact, many of history's well-known authors, inventors, artists, and scientists, if they were alive today, would be diagnosed with some form of "mental illness" or behavioral "disorder." The question becomes whether there are connections between creative or intuitive phenomena and altered states of consciousness, brain activity, and various personality and behavioral attributes that are routinely pathologized by today's psychological community.

That is not to minimize chemical imbalances in the brain or

cognitive impairment. To be sure, much progress has been made in the treatment of these ailments through medication and behavioral modification. However, the mysteries of the brain remain largely unexplored. Most of the time, when my son would describe what he was seeing and hearing, the inconsistencies in logic made it clear that something was amiss. However, there have been times when his perceptions were dead-on. His accuracy could be astonishing, which made me wonder if Steven's claims were correct and he *was* tapping into another dimension. Was he able to see beyond the veil?

These thoughts caused me to question my sanity. My intuitive abilities had always been strong, especially when it came to my sons, and that was even more pronounced with Steven. At times, my "mother's intuition" would kick in and I would "know" one of them was in trouble; or the phone would ring, and I would sense who it was before I looked at the caller ID. Perhaps, it was synchronicity, or maybe coincidence, but that inner voice was something I came to accept. I suspected everyone wrestled with their "voices": be it the inner critic, the "angel" or "devil" whispering in our ears, our mother's voice, our father's voice, or echoes of an abusive ex. Today, when I walk into a room and I am suddenly bombarded by the chatter of all of my insecurities, or when I start a project and find myself making a mental list of all the reasons why it will not work, I wonder if this is the same kind of internal noise Steven hears in each and every moment—only mine is less amplified and more manageable. At what point do inner battles take over outer realities, and when they do, what is it exactly that determines the line between sanity and insanity?

This fine line becomes blurrier in cases when one becomes obsessed with a lover, or injustice becomes an unhealthy fixation, or when an addiction takes over one's life. It is easier to ignore our own "crazy" when we consistently avoid individuals who do not follow social protocols, applying labels like "deviant, or "outcast" instead. Perhaps, social acceptance is the only real difference between us. If we can keep the mentally "ill" sidelined (either in prisons or hospitals, or on the peripheries in homeless shelters, encampments, or on the streets) then we do not have to think about them. More importantly, we do not have to face our own fragile proximity to madness. It is much more palatable to deflect, and to scapegoat "the homeless," or "those people" over in the seedy part of town behind the train station. What would happen if we began to see ourselves in the eyes of the outcast? What if we acknowledged we were not that different? What if we actually took the problems regarding mental health to task and refused to tolerate the impotence of the medical and judicial systems? The urge can be strong to crusade against the injustices that our broken systems perpetuate. However, when one is dependent on those services, the dilemma becomes much more problematic.

Although the mental health system in the United States is clearly inadequate, effective alternatives are much harder to come by than one might think. The very institutions I resented in the past have provided my son's care when I could not; they have housed, fed, medicated him, and for the most part, kept him safe. Nurses, doctors, attendants, social workers, and public defenders have worked diligently on his behalf; and even though Steven has endured unproductive treatments, poorly trained staff, and an uninspired justice system, by and large his care has been fair. My son has rarely expressed fear of or resistance to hospitalization. Still, many of the hospitals, residential treatment facilities, and jails where Steven has been housed function with limited supplies and funding. Staff are too often overworked and underpaid. Except for the times when he has been incarcerated, there have been only a few occasions when I was truly frightened that Steven would be hurt on the "inside." However, medication was another story.

It is terrifying to watch your child in the throes of psychosis, but the side-effects of antipsychotic medication can be just as devastating. I have seen Steven lethargic, unable to sit up or stay awake, drooling, trembling, and manic. He goes through various periods of weight loss and weight gain, which is one of the reasons he resists taking his meds. Steven's inability to speak clearly for the past five years is especially tragic, because he was such a gifted speaker and singer. Research suggests that his slurred speech is a result of tardive dyskinesia, a side effect that causes involuntary muscle spasms or a lack of muscle control. However, Steven's case seems to be unusual, and I have been unsuccessful advocating for a change in medication. Doctors, nurses, and staff do not have the benefit of seeing him at his best; they do not know how capable he is, and most assume he has a speech impediment. The professionals are skeptical that his slurred speech and inability to chew are side effects of the drugs, insisting that the paralysis in his tongue and spasms in his jaw are unrelated. I know better.

I became convinced about those side effects when Steven was court-ordered from the hospital into a homeless shelter in 2017. Two days later he called—his speech was completely restored. I was amazed. When I asked if he was taking his meds, he lied and told me he was, but I heard the mania in his voice. I knew he was off his medication and the cycle was beginning again. More to the point, my suspicions were confirmed: when he stopped taking his meds, he spoke clearly for the first time in over a year. Powerless to intervene in my son's case, I was (and still am) at a loss for what to do. As a musician, singer, and songwriter unable to use his voice, robbed of dexterity, and an inability to focus, Steven has lost an essential part of himself. Yet, his doctors are unwilling to consider alternatives to standard treatment, which appears to be nothing more than heavy sedation.

Even more discouraging, none of the medications Steven has been prescribed prevented his auditory or visual hallucinations. He is just less likely to act on them, or to care. It was Sarah who helped to explain these seemingly futile (and even damaging) courses of treatment. She had spent years taking antipsychotic drugs and antidepressants, and had successfully come through with no noticeable after-effects. This, I found to be reassuring. She shared how much anxiety and rage (due to frustration) could be produced in someone suffering from chemical imbalances in the brain. The heavy sedation, she explained, calmed the body enough so that the person affected did not hurt themselves or others. I saw the logic in that, but I was still troubled by what I saw as the fundamental problem: treating the symptoms instead of the cause of my son's condition.

As yet, scientists do not fully understand what causes these brain imbalances, but medical research for mental health has not been a priority. On so many levels, American ingenuity and innovation is unsurpassed, and if there were a collective demand (or rather, a financial incentive) to unravel the mysteries of the brain, no expense would be spared, no impasse would remain. Mental illness, however, isn't sexy or heartwarming enough to capture the public's attention. There is no poignant image of a suffering child, or sad, wet puppy mascot to rally around, nor are there marathon runs or ribbons, and only a handful of public figures or celebrities are willing to reveal their mental health challenges. More likely, mental imbalance becomes a spectacle, and a public fall from grace serves as media fodder, while an individual's professional and/or personal life implodes. Ours is a voyeuristic society that feeds on vicarious scandal and tragedy. Particularly in American culture, mental illness is ugly and anathema and, since a large percentage of those who suffer are indigent, they are deemed nothing more than a public nuisance.

I am not innocent or exempt. I experience the same revulsion when the disheveled woman on the subway mutters incoherently, or when the unmistakable odor of the homeless guy at the public library permeates my personal space. Like most people, I avoid eye contact and cross the street to bypass the "crazies." Then, I imagine all of the people who ignore my son, refusing to look him in the eye as he scrounges through a collection of cigarette butts at the entrance of a liquor store. In those moments, I feel compelled to take action. More than once, I have pulled over at a busy intersection to run into the median with whatever I could scavenge out of the backseat, handing it over to a vagrant with a cardboard sign reading, "Homeless. Anything will help!" Or, holding up traffic, I rummage through my backpack at a stoplight, desperate to find a stray $5 bill to give to a panhandler. I would like to say this is because I am a compassionate human being, but it's not.

Honestly, my motives are driven by grief. These occasions happen more frequently when Steven is out of touch and on the street—when I have no way of helping him or knowing if he is alive. Often, I am overcome by a need to stop and give whatever I can to homeless men his age (especially those who remind me of Steven). This comes from some irrational belief that if I give $5 or a blanket to one of these pseudo-Stevens, the "Universe" just might provide my son with something he needs five thousand miles away. This may sound crazy, but it is my way of coping.

In 2016, I had a brief experience of how mental illness might feel when I developed a brain infection as a result of Lyme disease. True, it was not the same as schizophrenia, but it revealed how frightening it is to lose one's cognitive abilities. For several weeks, I was unable to process written information. For a college professor, this was debilitating. Before I was diagnosed, my ability to complete certain tasks or maintain my routine became impaired. For example, one day I was so disoriented that I could not find my way out of a mall. This was not simply forgetting where I parked; I literally could not figure out how to get out of the building. I was terrified that I had Alzheimer's or early onset dementia. At times, my brain simply would not "load" information, much like computer lag while accessing a webpage. I was plagued with migraines for the first time in my life, manifesting all sorts of neurological symptoms that made me feel as if I was losing my mind. For months, I doubted whether I would recover, or if I would ever be "normal" again.

Truth be told, I am not the same.

It took more than a year for my brain to heal—to restore my ability to think, write, and organize thoughts (and locate my car in parking lots). Even though I recovered, I am still adapting to my "new brain." It just does not work the way it once did. I have limitations I did not have before, and I also have new and different sensitivities and perceptions. I consider myself fortunate not to be debilitated by Lyme disease, thanks to swift and effective medical treatment. Still, the powerful intravenous antibiotics I had to take caused me to question which was worse—the illness or the treatment. But I am grateful every day that modern medicine restored the health of my brain. If only the same could be said for Steven.

This experience gives me the ability to empathize with my son. I am acutely aware of how fragile sanity is, and how disorienting it can be when perceptions are out of balance. Of all the emotions I experienced during my illness, grieving the loss of my mental health was the most overwhelming. I understand more clearly Sarah's point about medication calming the body while imbalances in the brain are addressed. In my case, Lyme disease brought some important gifts—it was a tipping point for my personal growth. It caused me to reevaluate my life, embrace its blessings, nurture fulfilling relationships, and eliminate whatever was hindering my well-being. Most importantly, in some way, I am convinced that my illness led me to reunite with my son. My Underworld journey through the neurological crisis in my brain prepared me to meet Steven, if only briefly, in his realm.

This brings to mind an episode in the tale of Odysseus in Greek mythology,[10] and a brief encounter between the hero and his mother when he traveled to the Underworld to consult a prophet. The *Odyssey* is without a doubt a quintessential "hero's journey"—Odysseus battled for ten years in the Trojan War; he endured another ten years of trials before he returned to reclaim his throne. While he was away, despairing over her son's absence, Anticlea walked into the sea to her death. She was therefore condemned to the Underworld of Hades. Odysseus was guided to Hades as part of his quest. Once he arrived in the Underworld, at first he did not recognize his mother and therefore refused to acknowledge her. When he did recognize her, she reported the state of things back in Ithaca. Anticlea shared how she committed suicide, how his father lived as a derelict in a perpetual state of grief, and how his wife and son longed for his return. Realizing the gravity of the situation, the hero was anxious to make his way back home. When Odysseus tried to embrace his mother, he found she no longer inhabited a corporeal body, and he had to leave her behind in Hades.

Most people are familiar with Homer's *Odyssey*, but not much is discussed about this encounter between Odysseus and his mother. However, Odysseus' epic journey catalyzed his mother's more subtle descent into Hades after she took her own life. As a result, she was able to see her son once more, even if she could not touch him. Homer was hinting at something mysterious in this relationship between mother and child; their intersecting descents into the Underworld simultaneously united and separated them.[11]

When I was researching archetypes of the grieving mother, the 1997 television mini-series *The Odyssey*, directed by Andrey Konchalovsky came to my attention. A mythological interpretation lends a new appreciation for how grief is portrayed in the film. In a brief but powerful scene, the overwhelming emotions associated with profound grief are evident. Irene Papas, as Anticlea, is intent on taking her own life. Odysseus' wife Penelope and her maid are out of their minds as they resolutely make their way to the shores of Ithaca. Odysseus's mother cannot take suffering the loss of her son any longer; she is determined to take action, one way or another. If one recognized Anticlea's pain, the level of rage and despair portrayed by Papas was understandable. If not, the scene could seem overly dramatic. As a matter of fact, in the "Comments" section of a short clip found on YouTube, a group ridicules the women for what they deemed as poor acting. However, I understood the ferocity and madness they displayed.[12]

Without experiencing a similar agony, the emotional portrayals might seem exaggerated. Yet, Anticlea lost her will to live, because the grief over her son's absence was so intense that taking another breath seemed implausible. The YouTube "trolls" seemed but spectators, and could not empathize with the grieving mother. Most likely they had no frame of reference for Anticlea's pain—they had never encountered a sorrow that could leave a father on the floor in rags and drive a mother into the sea. If they had, their hearts might have broken watching that scene. Instead, they mocked and criticized.

I could not help but remember Anticlea in the Underworld as I grappled with my emotions each time I sat across from Steven feeling helpless and unable to connect. My heart resonated in solidarity with the keening women on the beach in the Konchalovsky film; I recognized

Anticlea's sacrifice, her primal passion, as she took matters into her own hands in order to meet her son in the Underworld. The only way to reach Odysseus and to urge him to return home, was to die. Then, she could remind him of his reality. Her story felt connected to the dream I had, and it caused me to wonder whether my brain infection was a kind of passage into the Underworld. Could it be that my hypersensitive brain could now tap into Steven's frequency, that I had been given the gift of a brief glimpse into his world? Could I, in a sense, meet him there in the depths, unable to reach, yet perhaps able to influence his path? It's thoughts like these that make me question my own sanity; but somehow they bring me comfort. Of this I am certain: my illness was an essential rite of passage—a catalyst—which caused me to face my fears. More importantly, it allowed me to see Steven and schizoaffective disorder with new eyes.

CHAPTER SIX

Remembering

Memory is a curious thing—like a holographic print one might find at a novelty shop. Standing off to one side or tilting it just the right way transforms an iridescent image or pattern into something entirely unrelated. A fractal design becomes a snow leopard—a lightning storm morphs into a waterfall. Memories are similar in form and expression. So, how can they be trusted? Without some confirmation or corroboration, how can one gauge their validity? But corroboration can be tricky, or altogether impossible. Most would agree that everyone is entitled to their own "take" and should "speak their own truth." One person's truth, however, may be another's dismembering—by this I mean that one interpretation may appear to discount the other's memory of the same event. One's remembrance may create a "dis-remembering" in another—a term I am using to indicate an active (yet, perhaps unconscious) forgetting. Sometimes, we choose to remember things a certain way, or to dis-remember parts of an experience out of an innate impulse to survive.

This is simply Psychology 101. Research shows that eyewitness accounts of the same event vary wildly. Memories are not static; they are alive, likely to be adapted to one's preferred version. If they are disturbing or traumatic, they may be suppressed. If a memory is not in line with one's self-image or worldview, it might be subconsciously altered in order to maintain a sense of continuity. Idealizing particular aspects of a memory may reinforce a desired self-image or outcome, but that will rarely correspond to how others see it.

This is where the waters become murky. The space between remembering and forgetting affects how truth is ascertained, especially in the case of family secrets. "Truth" is in perception, and perception is subjective, like dreams. Consider a dream—one may awaken terrified or thrilled—adrenaline surges, or perhaps a heavy sadness descends. But these physiological and emotional responses are not based on anything that *actually* happened. Trying to describe the dream to someone else is often impossible; even as one attempts to form the words, the details seem to dissolve. Still, dreams are "real" based on the responses they evoke in the dreamer. Occasionally, a portion of a dream may be retained: an insight, a feeling, or a recovered memory. In the waking state, what is left (the emotional or physiological response) indicates a kind of truth. So, is the dream/memory accurate? Do these emotional and somatic responses define the "truth" of the experience?

I remember the summer Steven took me for a ride in his 1987 Toyota Celica. When I reflect on it now, I realize it was the last time my son was lucid and "present" in a way that allowed us to truly connect. It was 2009, and he was proud to have saved his money to buy his first car. My maiden voyage was a bit of a shock, however, when he convinced me to ride along while he drove a friend to work. Skeptically, I climbed into the tiny back seat, not realizing that in a convertible, that is the last place anyone over the age of thirty should ride. Immediately, I felt as if I were in a wind tunnel, and all I could do was close my eyes and mutter a prayer, holding on for dear life, as my hair whipped wildly in all directions.

My ears hummed from the vortex, and I complained to Steven once he slowed enough to hear me. Good naturedly, he pretended not to hear: "How ya' doin' back there, Mom?" I couldn't help but laugh as he grinned in the rearview mirror.

Once the passenger seat was empty, I awkwardly pried myself from the back and climbed in next to him. The moment my son hit the highway, I knew I had to own a convertible. The open air, expansive sky, and the prairie unfolding before us was exhilarating. We cruised down the smooth state road, with the sun on our faces, his stereo blasting some groovy band he wanted me to hear. It was one of those perfect Midwestern summer days, when cicadas compose their soundtracks on the fly, and emerald fields of corn stretch on for miles. I relaxed into the sound of the wind and wheels on the pavement, Steven's playlist, and his unmistakable presence. He mused about life and possibilities, politics, and religion—brainstorming ideas for his new role as a guitar instructor. I savored this moment. He was twenty-two years old that summer (the same age as the Celica) and on top of the world. I wanted to believe he could have the promising life he was imagining for himself. He was beautiful, talented, and full of life.

One can so easily desire a specific reality, or become so attached to a particular idea of the way things should be, that objectivity is lost. Admittedly, a mother's perspective is biased; we see the best in our children. Naturally, I believe my sons are the most gifted, most handsome, most innovative men I know, each with their unique personalities and talents. No emotion compares to the love I have for each of them. This is what it means to be a mother.

Travis, my oldest son, was always the "golden boy." Everything he attempted, everything he touched, just seemed to work. I remember marveling at his grace and athleticism at a high school basketball game. Everyone saw it—as if he had wings and could fly. His ease on the court was one of the most elegant things I had ever seen. Travis was a talented musician too, sharing that gift with his brothers whose admiration was clear, even though they resented him with equal measure.

As siblings do, each thought the others got more attention. Travis, the big brother, fueled typical sibling rivalry—frustrating his brothers with privileges not afforded younger boys. To them, he seemed to be the one for whom everything came easily. Although he may have had an easier time socially, he internalized a lot of instability and hostility because he was older and more aware during the time when his father and I divorced. Because Travis was mature for his age, he was treated more like an adult, and although that was not always to his benefit, his brothers were convinced he was "the favorite."

For the two older boys, Devin was undoubtedly "the favorite." He was the "baby," and they complained that he "got away with" things they did not. It was probably true, since parents generally learn as they go, and after a third child are much more likely to choose their battles (partly out of wisdom, but mostly out of exhaustion). Devin struggled in the shadow of his accomplished oldest brother, and he had to compete with Steven, who had a way of demanding everyone's attention.

Steven was intense. He had a tendency to torment his brothers. A minor squabble usually escalated into all-out war. His energy could be so suffocating that it easily overwhelmed all of us. His brothers often ended up feeling like bystanders in the Steven spectacle. Though he was admittedly at the center of whatever drama was unfolding, he was not the only one who had a gift for instigating. When they weren't aggravating one another, the boys were conspiring to pull off some kind of caper.

Devin was a sensitive child, mercilessly teased and bullied by his brothers. They called him "Momma's boy" and criticized his every move. Despite incessant ridicule, he was resilient and fiercely loyal to his brothers. He was also the comedian in our family, and I had a very special bond with my silly, loving little boy. Around the age of nine, he began the inevitable rite of passage boys undertake: separation from their mothers. This was yet another loss that compounded my grief, and while it wasn't obvious, Devin's humor hid a deep well of sadness. As the youngest of three, he had to fight for his brothers' acceptance in addition to his parents' attention. Being labeled "the favorite" came at a high price for Devin.

Accusations of favoritism were inescapable. Unlike parents who insist they love all of their children the same, I admit, I love my sons differently. I had to learn to establish individual relationships with them in order to love them in ways unique to their personalities. Each required a different kind of mothering when they were young, and the same can be said today. Sadly, I have never been able to give any of them all they needed. Having three sons in the span of three and a half years meant I was pushed to the limit. From the moment they woke up in the morning, to the moment they collapsed at night, it was perpetual motion. Keeping three ravenous boys fed, clothed (when I could get them to wear them), and in one piece was a Herculean task.

I may have kept them intact physically, but I was unable to protect them emotionally. Their father and I were in survival mode, just trying to "get by." Frequently, he worked over ten hours a day, and most of the time, we had one car and no money. Lacking proper role models ourselves, we were clueless—guided only by our instincts (or lack thereof). I was reminded of this during more intake assessments than I can count, whenever Steven was hospitalized or started a new program. Reports might read: "lack of stability," "history of substance abuse," or "inadequate supervision."

It is hard to accept that children carry their psychological wounds as they mature, especially when parents must admit that they failed to prevent them, or face being the cause. These are bitter pills to swallow. Families are laden with burdens and secrets as it is; adding mental illness to the mix creates a unique code of silence, and a very complex set of family dynamics. My sons developed a troubled brotherhood. Yet, even a troubled brotherhood has its own form of solidarity. The boys have lived by this code, keeping many secrets between them. While some of those secrets have come to light, I'm afraid far too many skeletons remain hidden.

Children live in worlds entirely their own. Siblings in particular bond over shared encounters—the triumphs and the traumas. Theirs is a hidden world that often excludes parents. I realized this over dinner one night when my adult sons described a time Steven jumped into a flooded creek to come to Devin's aid after he was swept off of the road by rushing water. They recounted another time when Travis fell through the ice while walking on a pond. I was speechless. Then, my heart stopped when Devin shared how his brothers held his head under the water until he was sure he would drown. Why did I not know this? How many times had they faced death together, or tried to kill each other? Their love/hate relationships seemed marked by the alternating desire to murder one another and a willingness to risk their lives to protect the other.

Friends from large families would chuckle when I described the chaos of raising three rowdy boys. They assured me the constant bickering and fighting were "normal." I was unconvinced and bewildered. My memories of this time contain an element of anxiety; many things I don't remember at all. As an only child who did not make friends easily, I had no idea how to handle my sons' behavior. True, there were moments of comradery and wonder. But those brief periods were often cut short by Steven's erratic behavior. Even when Travis and Devin tried to include or protect him, ultimately they had to retreat in order to get out of the way of his locomotive mania. We have all had to realize that you can't lay on the train tracks to stop the train.

Steven was not to blame. At the time, we had no idea to what extent our lives would be altered, or the unfathomable grief that lay ahead. While the enormity of mental illness has had a devastating effect on our family, it was the perfect storm. Many things contributed to life as it was, and everyone tried to cope as best they could. There were happy moments, but those were too often eclipsed by uncertainty, drama, and loss on many levels.

It is an ongoing process to forgive, especially to forgive oneself. Accepting the way things were helps to accept the way things are; acceptance restores one's peace of mind. It has a way of "re-storying" the tragedy of it all. Part of this restoration has been to validate my sons' stories as they tell them. Their stories are not my stories, and the stories don't need to agree. In time, I have learned to separate our experiences of the past. I am able to validate my sons without invalidating my own experience. Laying these stories down, next to each other, is how we begin to forgive. Forgiveness and acceptance lead to gratitude—gratitude for all of the pain *and* all of the joy we shared over the years.

Years after my joyous ride in Steven's convertible, I finally bought my own: a used red and black 1994 Geo Tracker, the car I dreamt of for years, but did not believe I would ever own. It became the symbol of my emerging identity and purpose, which was fitting, since that car was a ridiculous, impractical rattletrap. The Tracker was a crazy little tank that refused to quit even as the frame rusted out from under it; I loved it!

Around the same time, Steven was heading West on his quest for adventure. His brothers had their own families—Travis and his wife were living in the Midwest with a new baby, and Devin was raising his son. Back in New England, I relished my jouncey rides, remembering moments like the one with Steven in the summer of '09. I reminisced about a time when three pint-sized cyclones consumed every waking thought. Some of my favorite memories they seem to have forgotten: bathing in a spring-fed river, spooning no-bake cookies onto sheets of wax paper, scrounging up 25¢ for a loaf of bread to feed the swans, collecting peacock feathers and gooseberries, popping corn and watching thunderstorms roll in, and bedtime serenades with songs I wrote on my guitar. This, I remember; I have hope—maybe someday they will too.

CHAPTER SEVEN

The Maestro

Stories come in unpredictable ways. For me, their presence has provided stability in the disorientation and dissolution of my own Mother/s Odyssey. Guiding "angels," with their own heartbreaking tales of loss, often showed up unannounced—like my friend Jaffa, who stayed with me during a severe emotional storm, and my island companion Sarah, who tempered my isolation and despair with her message of resilience and hope. Their stories became anchor points as my own continued to unfold.

Others, in a sense, became stories within my story. Their lessons have taken time to take root, and their players have had less obvious roles. They were more like featured artists in the symphony of life, playing unnoticed for a time; then stepping forward with a display of other-worldly talent so captivating, they were the epitome of transcendence. So it was for Levon, who taught me to suspend the rational, refashion my beliefs about mental illness, and remain open to the mysterious and extraordinary.

It was around 2004 when I met him while living in a small town in the Midwest. My sons were blossoming into men, and I was working on my Bachelor's degree at a nearby college. Levon gave private guitar lessons to students on campus, installing himself on one of the park benches scattered across the lawn. I had been curiously watching him for several weeks before I finally approached the striking older gentleman about studying the guitar. Although I was certain I lacked the aptitude, Levon disagreed. I was insecure about teaching myself to play on the honey-toned Yamaha my mother had left behind decades before. While I did not become one of his prize pupils, Levon and I developed a lasting friendship. He became an important father-figure, even though his old-school ways made him more grandfatherly than fatherly.

Truly, the man was (and still is) an enigma, on a spectrum somewhere between saint and savant (or perhaps, swindler and sage). I called him the "Maestro," because there was something about him that not only commanded admiration, but hearkened back a couple of centuries. This was also because many of his guitar pieces were written by the masters: Mozart, Bach, and Beethoven. More than that, Levon looked the part of a classical era composer striding down the sidewalk a few blocks from the university, one arm bearing a well-worn guitar case, and a black spray-painted coffee can under the other. The shock of white hair curled at his collar gave him an old world sensibility. In his characteristic white dress shirt, black slacks, and lace-up shoes, he was a distinctive figure. No matter what time of year, no matter what was on his schedule, this was Levon's "uniform." The only addition was a black blazer or a mid-calf black wool coat and scarf in cold weather. A slight smirk played along the corners of his mouth, and the Maestro's grey/blue eyes twinkled as if he was always contemplating an inside joke.

It was clear that Levon could have been diagnosed with some type of "mental illness" if he gave any credit to Western psychology (which he did not). He had found a way to fly under the radar, riding the line between dignity and disrepute. He did not drive and did not hold a traditional job, living instead on gigs and tips at coffee houses, restaurants, or day spas. He gave lessons on a variety of stringed instruments, as well as the piano. On any given day, if Lady Luck was smiling (and breakfast was on the menu at the venue where he was playing), he scored a meal "on the house," or an enamored patron would pick up the tab. Since his income was inconsistent, and living arrangements were always sketchy, the Maestro often relied on his students for transportation, lodging, or attending to business matters. More than once, he needed an eleventh hour rescue from eviction or some other crisis. Mundane activities were not Levon's strong suit. He was preoccupied with practicing, teaching, and composing, or he was schmoozing a recording session at some local studio, ever-touting his forthcoming debut album as a world-renowned classical guitarist.

His stories were legendary, but I could never tell if he was serious: tales of him teaching Mel Bay everything he knew, Bob Dylan praising his technique, or holding court with all the "greats" in Greenwich Village in the 60s. Then, there were the other times, times when I had no idea what he was saying. He spoke in riddles, so convincingly, I was certain I was missing something, perplexed by his strangely coded monologues, which were peppered with blatant grandiosity, wise counsel, apocalyptic paranoia, and an infectious giggle that seemed slightly askew. On the other hand, Levon's guitar playing was celestial, delicate, and precise; there was something both divine and disturbing about him.

Our friendship evolved over time, and I learned to accept the Maestro's idiosyncrasies. Although I was his student for only a brief period, I appreciated his teaching method, which dismantled self-imposed limitations and poor instruction from the past. He used a subtle flank approach—distracting students with stories, while suggesting slight adjustments to hand positions, instructing in short bursts, and then requiring pupils to set the guitar aside for a few moments before beginning the pattern all over again. I experienced this for myself, and looked on as students learned in spite of themselves.

Eventually, I urged Steven, who was eighteen at the time and seventeen-year-old Devin, as they were developing their own musical talents, to take lessons from Levon. He was nothing but patient, whereas, my role became more practical. I drove the Maestro to the convenience store where he bought and redeemed his lottery tickets with religious fervor. He insisted he could "play the numbers" with astounding accuracy using his own method. If that were the case, I wondered why he was frequently in financial trouble. There were timely "wins" when a bill was due or his electricity was about to be turned off. However, he seemed unable to manifest a windfall "on demand," though he insisted he could if he wanted. As the months passed, Levon became a part of our lives, coming to dinner once or twice a week, and I sometimes washed his clothes and ironed his shirts. The Maestro had an unassuming air that inspired dedication from his "disciples."

Our relationship was not one-sided, though. He counseled me when I faced parenting dilemmas as my sons became more and more independent, and he was a guide and confidant as I began my journey from Midwest girl to Harvard grad. Although Levon was a skilled astrologer, developing charts for local patrons, his prophetic skills did not interest me at the time. But when he assured me that I would be accepted if I took a long shot and completed the application for a graduate program, I applied to Harvard Divinity School. As a Midwest native, making my way to Harvard felt like something akin to *The Wizard of Oz*; indeed, Dorothy on her way to the Emerald City. But Levon was adamant, and in 2007, just as he predicted, I received my acceptance letter.

Even more uncanny than his prediction was his connection to the Northeast, which would become my new home once I began grad school. Travis and Steven were embarking on their own journeys into adulthood, and Devin was living with his father over a thousand miles away. Now was the time for me to step into the unknown and explore this next phase of life.

Levon had lived in Cambridge decades before, playing guitar along Massachusetts Avenue (colloquially known as "Mass Ave"), just as he had in the university town about thirty miles from the college where we met. Though a completely different culture, it had a similar vibe—with its own "Mass Ave," hookah bar, bookstores, and art galleries. Levon tried to prepare me for the culture shock I would face with stories that made Cambridge seem slightly less like the mythical Emerald City than I was sure it would be. He advised where to rent, and discouraged anything short of a full-on embrace of the opportunities coming my way.

It was a strange synchronicity that I met Levon with his ties to Cambridge in a lazy, Midwestern town just before I found myself thrust into this unfamiliar iconic landscape with its archaic brick streets, and all the pretense and posturing of academia. His accounts of Cambridge had the same surreal quality they always had. However, the fantastical stories of Greenwich Village now shifted to playing guitar at Cafe Algiers on Brattle Street for room and board, rubbing elbows with all sorts of colorful personalities, and collecting an assortment of allies and champions at outdoor Sunday morning services in Harvard Square. There was a queer consistency to his life that made it both believable and unbelievable—mostly unbelievable.

Case in point: a couple of years after my relocation to Cambridge, to my astonishment, I spotted Levon sitting in the window of Au Bon Pain, a well-known coffee shop in Harvard Square, which I passed nearly every day between classes. In complete disbelief, I entered to find him chatting up a captivated customer. He had spontaneously made his way from the Midwestern Mass Ave to Mass Ave in Cambridge, with the promise of a regular gig at Cafe Algiers.

This is how it's been with Levon; he has become a permanent figure in my life. Bypassing typical lines of communication, we rarely speak on the phone, and I have only written a letter once or twice over the years. Mysteriously, we are able to connect if we are in close proximity. So, even though I was dumbfounded to find the Maestro sipping coffee on Mass

Ave right across from "The Coop," the infamous Harvard bookstore, I shouldn't have been all that surprised.

Levon did not remain in Cambridge; things went downhill—the gig did not pan out, and promises of a room for rent never materialized. A vagabond life was not as he remembered, perhaps because he was older and people were much more disconnected than they were "back in the day." In his past life, he was always able to score a room, a gig, and a meal. Times had changed. The Harvard Square he remembered was no more; he could no longer count on the kindness of strangers to get by.

At that time, I was going through my own personal disintegration, intensified by the pressure of Ivy-league expectations and my difficulty adapting to New England. My second marriage was coming to an end, I failed an exam for the first time in my life, and I began yet another Master's program in a different part of the city. I lost touch with Levon, learning months later that he summoned one of his protégés to ferry him to more welcoming Mass Ave territory back home.

A couple of years later I went home to visit, and was passing through, with only one afternoon to spend. I was told the Maestro could be found at a certain coffee shop off of 23rd Street near the local campus. Sure enough, within twenty minutes of placing my order, Levon walked in with his latest disciple. He had landed on his feet as always, living in a basement apartment owned by his most recent benefactor. The Maestro was working on his recordings, which he said were "next level," and we seemed to pick up in mid-conversation with a warmth and familiarity I experience with few people.

The next time I saw him was in the summer of 2017: same Levon, different coffee shop. It had been twelve years since we first met, but in all the years I had known him, he had not aged. In fact, in some ways he seemed to get younger as time passed. I listened to his elaborate tales. Some I could follow; others were in his cryptic style. I didn't try to de-code them, I just enjoyed his presence, contemplating our synchronistic relationship and the unpredictable ways people arrive in each other's lives, and how the most unlikely characters come to teach, guide, and influence us.

Everything about the Maestro was a paradox. He was a part-time vagrant who took up residence in one's heart; at least he had in mine. He was every bit the trickster, slyly slipping in and out of identities—from innocent child to seasoned master. His demeanor was generally upbeat, but I saw him cloud over with an ominous mood now and then. Levon refused to play by the rules, but was disciplined in his musicianship. He was a worldly philosopher and at times, a willful fool. To the fullest extent, the Maestro embodied what it meant to be human. Yet, there were times when I was convinced he was not of this world: when he "read" people with remarkable intuition, or when he cursed some "evil" perpetrated against him with brooding intensity, or when I walked into a coffee shop after not seeing him in years and he launched into *Asturias*, my favorite piece. He did this with angelic ease, his intricate runs evoking pure ecstasy. All the while, the Maestro smirked over the swell of his guitar, one foot propped on a matte black coffee can, his devilish grin playing in the margin between derelict and divine.

Such duality is common in individuals who straddle two worlds. Levon will always be an enigma, and I have encountered others with a similar disposition—usually artists, shamans, and seers of one kind or another. Steven somehow reminds me of Levon, yet my son seems not to have learned how to navigate the divide; he is bewildered, unable to differentiate the mundane world from the web of his psyche. Steven does not appear to realize when he is lucid and when he is not. The Maestro, on the other hand, does not much care whether or not he is making sense to anyone. He is confident (and arrogant)—those who do not understand what he is saying are the ones with the problem. Levon has always seemed privy to some secret knowledge that is lost on the rest of us.

This seems a reasonable assumption, since he does have preternatural abilities. The Maestro thrives in his mantic presence, composing sonatas and sonnets like some throwback Master of the Queen's music or Poet Laureate. Though he seems a bit of a necromancer, Levon is pragmatic and matter-of-fact, using mathematical logic, complete with formulas and systems to generate his own luck. I never knew him to attribute anything to "voices" or "messages," or any sort of divine providence. Instead, Levon appears to "calculate" information with savant-like accuracy. He is able to use the information that comes to him rather than being swept away by it.

When Steven confided in me about hearing people's thoughts while he was working as a guitar instructor at the music store, this was the point at which our paths diverged. Mother's intuition and whatever personal battles I had waged paled in comparison to what he was describing. I stood by helplessly as my son was swept out to the proverbial sea, a sea of confusion and isolation. Repeatedly, he asked whether I was appearing to him in dreams or sending him psychic messages. I assured him I was not, but he was skeptical. Ten years later, he brought it up again while I was visiting him in Hawai'i.

I wondered from time to time if I had become a sort of permanent specter in Steven's experience, in the same way that many of us contend with our mother's voice, a disembodied "voice" that might comfort or criticize. Had I become an ever-present character in my son's mind? For Steven, voices became personified, and he seemed unable to discern whether they were "real," or coming from his own psyche. I considered that he might be hearing the typical mental "clutter" we all experience, but on an amplified level. Did he simply lack the ability to manage his mental activity? Even more sobering: What if Steven had an ability to pick up on my subconscious worries and fears? Was I inadvertently terrorizing my son because he could hear my thoughts?

Over the years, my observations led me to recognize a pattern— individuals who have tendencies toward mental "illness," those who might be characterized as "differently-abled" (or whatever definition one cares to use), at times seem to exist in a realm where the "veil" is thinner between worlds than it is for the rest of us. Is it possible they (like the Maestro and Steven), could be tuned into frequencies imperceptible to most people? We all experience brief moments of synchronicity, or a feeling comes over us, a premonition. Perhaps we are "tuned in" to a loved one many miles away, or we receive an inexplicable warning, or know exactly when to call a friend. Generally, a moment like this is considered a coincidence. But is it, really? What if these kinds of "radio waves," so to speak, were magnified—deafening, in fact—for people like my son?

Maybe this is the case for the Maestro and Steven, except my son lacks the understanding and training to sort through what he "receives." Shamans, prophets, healers, artists—all must find a way to channel information productively. I would speculate that those without context for the impressions and images they experience live in a kind of psycho-spiritual exile, adrift and disoriented. Maybe they act out impulsively, engage in self-destructive behaviors, or become aggressive because they are overwhelmed by sensory input. If this barrage of information they tap into appears random or chaotic, it could be confusing and extremely frightening. In today's society, there is little tolerance for unconventional ways of perceiving the world. More likely than not, behaviors that don't "fit" are pathologized and medicated.

I don't know if Steven can tap into my thoughts, but it wouldn't surprise me. Just in case, I try to remain vigilant about anxiety and fear, since it is unproductive for me and potentially stressful for him. Scientists do not dispute the fact that thoughts are in fact electric impulses occurring within energetic fields that emanate from our bodies. If my son is hyper-sensitive to these impulses, there is little that I can do to help him. The only thing I can do is minimize my own negative, obsessive, or fear-based thoughts, which might transmit an anxiety-producing frequency.

For years, I worked closely with a shaman, hoping to find ways to help Steven. Even though I sought him out for my son, he taught me many difficult lessons. One thing he repeated again and again was "Thoughts. Words. And deeds." This was a signal to pay attention to the things that were within my control, release that which was not, and to stop entertaining negativity in any form. Ultimately, this was and still is the only way I can help my son.

I use several strategies to manage my worry, fear, and regret. Prayer and meditation are effective, as are 12-step techniques I learned over the years, and the Buddhist concept of non-attachment is particularly helpful. But, the most important lesson I have learned is that, regardless of where my sons are on their journeys, I can only live *my* life as fully as possible. Does this mean I am disengaged? No. Does it mean I am not concerned, or that I don't hold vigil for them when they are lost or troubled? Of course not. What it means is that I cultivate the most empowered, compassionate, and authentic version of myself that I possibly can. In this way, the frequency I emit is the purest intentional transmission of love I have to offer.

This concept, in some form or another, is found in most religious traditions and spiritual paths. Some might call it prayer, or communion, or meditation. Being "in tune" creates a harmonic resonance more powerful than any other action one can take. It is a kind of "soul symphony," and I find I am my own "maestro," composing and conducting the most important symphony of all. This imperceptible sound (wave) reaches across the expanse, transcending time and space to touch the souls of my sons no matter where they are. This is prayer. This is unconditional love. This is living grief.

CHAPTER EIGHT

Questing

Each time I visited Steven at the hospital, he would have a list of requests at the ready. Since I was navigating the island for the first time, these "requests" were more like "quests." I was accustomed to ferreting out items for my son. Whenever he was in a facility that allowed him to receive mail, he would compose a list of things he wanted. Once he set his sights on them, he would not let up until his packages arrived. Gathering up all of the things he wanted and sending them in a timely manner created a tremendous amount of stress. Sometimes, I felt conflicted about purchasing the items he asked for; most of the time I was just relieved to accomplish one more task. I came to dread interactions with the postal clerk and the questions these packages raised.

"Hawai'i, huh?"

"Yes. They're for my son. He lives there."

"Wow! That must be great. What are you doing here in the Northeast, when you could live in paradise?"

I would smile and nod my head with my heart in my throat. Inside, I was shouting: "Seriously? Do you not see the hospital's name written on the label, you ignorant ass?"

Now, I was on the island, and one of Steven's requests was particularly challenging: *Magic* cards. The problem was, I didn't really know what I was looking for or where to find them. Steven had been focused on *Magic: The Gathering* for more than a year. Even though I felt role-playing games were a useful tool, I was skeptical about these cards, because Steven took the magical powers and creatures described on them literally. A few months earlier, I had resisted sending the decks he wanted. However, a doctor and case manager at one of the facilities where he was housed suggested I send them as a coping strategy for his anxiety. Reluctantly, I trudged to the Post Office and shipped a set of what I hoped were the right cards after watching several tutorials trying to understand this elaborate game that seemed geared mostly toward young people.

Steven said the first set I bought was too "demonic." So, I tried again, looking for what he called "righteous" magic cards. In the middle of the night, I would scroll online through an endless selection of *Magic: The Gathering* decks (*MTG*) trying to comprehend what he wanted. When I questioned whether they might feed into Steven's delusions, his case manager assured me that he was primarily holding and shuffling them. Knowing his obsession with "evil," magic, and the entities that appeared to him, I felt uneasy about providing anything that might pull him further from reality. However, I was even more conflicted about having to "police" his requests. After wrestling with the *Magic* card decision for weeks, I decided to say my piece to the professionals in charge and leave it in their hands.

Steven received Social Security Disability, and could requisition funds from his payee for whatever he wanted. Most of his requests reminded me of adolescent Steven: a *Dungeons and Dragons* spell book, candy (or sugar in any form), comic books, and name-brand clothing. But he was an "adult," and it wasn't my job to tell him what he could and couldn't buy with his own money. For years, I had been powerless to interrupt the cycle that was characteristic of mental "illness": homelessness, incarceration, hospitalization, medication, repeat. Not only was it no longer my responsibility to make decisions for my son, I had created a delicate balance of non-attachment and loving support, which was the only thing standing between me and what felt like an impending breakdown. The days of having to monitor his every move and enforce parental boundaries had long passed. In recent years, distance helped to keep my desire to "fix" Steven's situation mostly in check. This new island courier role, however, threatened to destabilize all of my coping strategies.

A year before I came to Oahu, Steven began to ask for "Under Armour," a trendy brand of athletic wear and underwear. I was puzzled as to why he was so insistent about it. Under Armour was pricey, and based on experience, I hesitated to buy anything of value for my son. Whatever I bought for him had to be, in a sense, "disposable." Many times, I would ship his requests only to find he had been relocated before he received them—and the facilities housing my son were not in the habit of forwarding packages after a client moved on. Other times, he would give belongings away when leaving one facility for another, because the rules would often change, or he was not allowed to take them with him. If he did receive items I bought for him, upon his release, they were usually stolen or lost within a matter of days. So, I was less than motivated to spend a significant amount of money (or time) procuring brand-name clothes for my wayward son. As the time neared for me to come to the island, Steven requisitioned a check so I could shop for whatever he wanted while I was there.

This seemed like a good idea at the time (he could spend *his* money on whatever he wanted). However, as I made my way to the hospital for our first visit, I quickly realized how challenging it would be. Steven wanted Arby's for lunch that day. After searching for the eatery closest to the hospital, I found one located at a mall about fifteen miles away. Between the outrageous traffic, the convoluted parking, and completely unfamiliar territory, my anxiety was high. It took an eternity to park, find a directory, and locate Arby's on the second level. After picking up Steven's food, on the verge of tears, I made my way back through the crowded mall out into the blazing heat.

I was going to see my son for the first time in six years. He asked specifically for cans or bottles of root beer since hospital regs banned unsealed containers. I had to make a second stop near the hospital for Steven's root beer and candy request. Panic set in when I got lost and couldn't find the grocery store. So, I settled for a mini-mart. Relieved that the mini-mart gods smiled upon me, I emerged with two cold cans of root beer and Reese's peanut butter cups. Traffic was worse than I expected. Frazzled and out-of-breath, I arrived at the hospital thirty minutes late with melted chocolate, warm root beer, and Steven's curly fries getting soggier by the minute.

I tried to hide my anxiety from my son. He seemed pleased, not minding the lifeless curly fries and melted candy, but that didn't change the fact that I felt completely demoralized. Each time we met, Steven had a list of things he wanted me to bring to our next visit, which he frequently changed during a last minute phone call. For five weeks, I worried over these lists. Every request felt like a life or death matter, and I had little control over my emotions. One afternoon, while combing the candy aisle in a local Walmart, when I couldn't find the Shock Tarts Steven asked for, I wanted to scream: *"My son wants Shock Tarts! Where are the Shock Tarts? What is wrong with you people!?"*

The first two weeks of this emotional roller coaster were brutal. Keeping the firestorm building inside of me at bay was exhausting. Rationally, I understood—I was a mother trying to provide for her son. I also knew his requests weren't "needs," but "wants" (mere luxuries), but it was the first time in ages that I had any measure of control when it came to Steven. So, I was obsessed with these tasks, wanting to provide for my son, but also to please him. Then, the requests became more challenging:

"Mom, could you go to Barnes and Noble at the Ala Moana Mall—back on the shelf near the bathroom, you'll find the sci-fi and fantasy section. Will you buy four or five *Star Trek* books? Make sure they are not part of a series."

"Hey Mom, they sell Under Armour clothes at Macy's. Please get some boxer briefs, a hoodie (with the string removed), and three long-sleeve undershirts."

"Mom, will you look for t-shirts with superheroes on them?"

"You can find *Magic* card booster packs at Walmart. Could you pick up three or four?"

"I need a CD player with headphones and some CDs: Jack Johnson, Stain'd, and some cool jazz. But make sure they don't have parental advisories."

"Hey Mom, could you look for some books on Greek mythology, but with not too much text and lots of pictures. Oh, and look for coloring books with Greek gods in them?"

I stared blankly at each list, a knot forming in the pit of my stomach.

My third weekend in Hawai'i was spent hunting down the latest set of requests. Steven asked me to go to Ala Moana Mall, because it was his "territory," where he spent so much time near Chinatown. As I drove toward the mall, I passed homeless encampments and city blocks that were much less dazzling than glitzy Ala Moana Boulevard. The mall was a tourist haven, drawing travelers from all over the world. Income disparity is never more in one's face than at the intersection of Saks Fifth Avenue and a tent village. Steven would ask if I noticed a certain park, or direct me to places where he liked to hang out, telling me where he scored free refills on soft drinks using discarded cups. He told me about a convenience store where he harvested cigarette butts from the outdoor ashtrays, breaking them up to roll his own cigarettes with pilfered rolling papers. As I guided my rental car through the maze of streets, shops, and pedestrians, I was inundated with sensory overload, the unrelenting crowds, and my heightened emotional state—I was in no mood for sightseeing. The blatant homelessness was disturbing, to be sure. But this mega-mall was too much for my recovering brain to handle post-Lyme disease, and my son had no way of knowing that I avoided these places at all costs.

I managed to navigate through downtown Honolulu to the massive parking garage at Ala Moana, but this was not a mall, it was a metropolis. I imagined Steven milling about in the cavernous parking garage, roadways and walkways intersecting and diverging in a web of consumerism. In my mind's eye, I saw him sleeping on benches, slipping into a store to use the bathroom, scoping out opportunities to score food, or anything he could trade on the street. His was a life I could not fathom, but somehow this first-hand experience allowed me to see it from my son's perspective. His descriptions of Ala Moana were enthusiastic, if not wistful. This was his "home." It was also where he had been arrested for shoplifting a radio at Walmart, sparking the latest round of court dates, jail time, and hospitalizations.

I found the Under Armour boxer briefs and two long-sleeved undershirts, which by some stroke of luck, happened to be in a department store within sight of the bookstore. Not bad, considering Ala Moana was four stories tall, covering a massive city block. I ordered Steven's books on Greek mythology online and had them delivered to Barnes and Noble, and was able to pick them up easily enough. I did not have as much luck finding the hoodie and superhero shirts. I headed north about ten miles, where I knew traffic and the crowds were more manageable—a bit out of the way, but worth it. By this time, I was frazzled but gratified that I had accomplished most of what was on his list.

After a brief trip to the grocery store to pick up that day's menu items—a salad with dried cranberries, root beer, and salt and vinegar potato chips—I stopped at the guard station, where a uniformed official called the nurses' station on Steven's unit. A message came back that "Environmentals" were underway, and I would have to come back in thirty minutes. I fumed, choking back how insignificant I felt inside this "System," subject to the whim of the overseers who decided whether or not I could see my son.

In that moment, my adrenaline spiked as the anxiety-fueled momentum of the entire weekend came to a standstill. The accomplished list of tasks, and all of my emotional calisthenics created what felt like a pressure-cooker in my head. The only option was to turn my car around, while gritting my teeth to keep from taking my rage out on the innocent guard. I drove aimlessly. Seething, my mind raced: maybe they weren't going to let me see him at all; perhaps, something had gone terribly wrong and they were in the process of some elaborate cover-up. I became convinced that something terrible had happened to my son.

On cue and a bit deflated, I returned to the hospital, arms loaded with purchases and all the receipts, which had to be turned in to Steven's social worker. Most times, the staff was polite while they screened my parcels and used an electronic wand to check for contraband. "Really? Do you think I have a file in my shoe?" I thought to myself. Occasionally, one of the more militant attendants would adopt a tone that reminded me of my place—I did not rank, not even a little.

As luck would have it, on this day, a more restrained nurse begrudgingly led me through the security routine, finally escorting me to where Steven waited in the hall. We entered the oppressive room reserved for guests. A staff member looked on as Steven glanced through my purchases. Then, they were gathered up and taken to be logged in at the nurses' station. All food was carefully inspected, and we were left alone.

Steven devoured his salad and potato chips, despite his difficulty chewing and swallowing. We made brief small talk but, mostly, he muttered to himself and was distracted. I prattled on about my treasure hunt at the mall, but he acknowledged me with only brief comments, immersed in reading the ingredients listed on the salt and vinegar potato chips. I asked if he wanted to play cards but, after about twenty minutes, he said he "just wasn't up for it today." I assured him that was okay, returning back down the hall from where I had come. When we reached the glass-enclosed attendant's desk, Steven kept walking without looking back or saying goodbye. "See ya' later, babe," I called after him. The nurse handed me my keys and unlocked two sets of doors and the metal gate, and that was that. I was dismissed.

Abruptly thrust into the parking lot, I numbly passed a hen with her peeping clutch of chicks. I had grown accustomed to the stray chickens and cats roaming the island and enjoyed the novelty. Mongooses slinking around dumpsters and trash bins, on the other hand, always startled me. Today, I was unfazed as they scavenged a few yards from this week's rented Toyota Corolla. Once in the safe zone of the car's interior, I stared at the bay trying to absorb the past forty-eight hours, but I was unable to process anything at all. My emotional freeway was still—I hit the wall.

Something had to change. I simply could not sustain this level of anxiety; it was not healthy and I didn't want to anymore. I felt that I was going to come apart as my ego played the victim card: "Look at all I am going through!" "After everything I've done, how can this be happening to me?" Why doesn't Steven appreciate how much I am doing for him?" "Don't these people realize *I am his mother?*"

I drove back down the mountain, trying to decide if I should limit my visits with Steven, but I could not do that. I was only on the island for a short period of time, and I did not know when (or if) I would see my son again. "What did you expect?" I asked myself. I didn't know the answer. All I knew was that all of the work I had done learning how to cope with Steven's schizoaffective disorder had gone by the wayside. I was back at square one.

Over the next few days, I reevaluated my expectations. It was not reasonable to assume Steven would (or could) acknowledge my presence or my efforts. I had to make a decision about how I would respond to his requests. So, I decided to think of them as "quests," to embrace the challenge, and to consider them adventures. I reminded myself to separate my need for validation from the reality of the situation. This reduced a lot of stress, and helped me to remember that my anxiety was self-imposed.

The next quest involved *Magic* cards. Since I was unable to find them elsewhere, I did some research and found an *MTG* trading store nearby. My new perspective was certainly put to the test as I tried to locate the tiny shop amidst the Harbor Center district in Aiea. Row after row of stores became a dizzying labyrinth of loading docks, corrugated metal storefronts, and a mish mash of parking spaces aligned this way and that. I found myself on a second floor open-air walkway passing what looked like several sparsely frequented businesses before finding The Durdle Zone nestled in a far corner. With no one in sight, I was surprised to find a green neon "Open" sign illuminating the window. As I approached the door, I was sure I would be the only walk-in customer they had seen in days, maybe weeks. I could not have been more wrong.

When I opened the door, I was struck by the murmurs vibrating throughout the space. The room was packed with card tables and banquet tables surrounded by young people immersed in some kind of gaming event. I wanted to turn around to make an escape, but I had come this far. Simply locating the store had been an ordeal; I could not turn back now. At the far end of the room, I spotted what looked like a sales counter. The back wall was covered with cards of every imaginable type and all manner of gaming paraphernalia.

Behind the cash register, a young man who looked like he was twelve did his best to decipher what I wanted—it was obvious I had no idea. He stayed patient in the midst of the hubbub, and I resisted the urge to bolt. I had invaded some sacred gaming territory. The goth-looking youth placated me with a couple of booster packs of *Magic* cards, fulfilling Steven's request. I was much too uncomfortable to revel in my achievement. I shoved some money at him and retreated back through the crowded room.

Even though I was unnerved by the whole encounter, I was triumphant as I returned to my car. Adopting my new quest perspective was helpful. I thought about the community of enthusiastic gamers I had witnessed. Most were in their teens and early twenties, and though the clerk who waited on me was polite, he clearly did not know what to do with an older mom-type on his home turf. Even so, I was intrigued by whatever was happening at The Durdle Zone, and appreciated the organization and community that was happening there. I also saw how *Magic the Gathering* functioned, likely as it was intended, and I wondered if Steven had ever been a part of such a community, or if he would be welcome. Were these his people? Or would he always be an outlier?

When I arrived for my visit with Steven later that day, he was decked out in the goods from my last quest: a royal blue, long-sleeved Under Armour undershirt beneath a grey Avengers t-shirt. He commented several times how much he liked them and thanked me profusely. Then, he explained how the "Under Armour" made him feel safe. With his tendency toward literal interpretation, I realized, he was not focused on the brand, but the message; this was Steven's motivation. He told me the superhero shirts channeled super powers to protect him.

Suddenly, it all made sense. My quests were more than just an inconvenient ordeal. I had been on a mission to retrieve my son's "armour," to provide him with the resources he needed to safeguard himself. What seemed like frivolous requests actually had purpose: the clothes were a shield, heroes gave him strength to fight his enemies, and the cards contained protective spells. He explained that the Greek gods helped him counter the dark voices, as did his carefully selected music choices. He scrutinized song lyrics, and while they seemed harmless to me, he believed they carried evil messages. The intricate mosaic of my son's mind began to unfold. I understood.

Although Steven's former case manager and psychiatrist encouraged me to send the *Magic* cards as a coping strategy many months before, the professionals at his current location did not agree. Like me, they questioned whether the cards exacerbated Steven's psychosis. At first, I did not realize that his cards had been confiscated. He had avoided the subject when he showed me a few of his favorites secreted away between the pages of his pocket New Testament. However, the subject came up when he asked me to smuggle in some booster packs containing ten to fifteen random cards. I was torn. Nevertheless, I didn't hesitate to undertake the quest to find The Durdle Zone. And I have to admit, I found an undeniable satisfaction in hiding the contraband cards under a thick stack of napkins at the bottom of a bag of tacos and burritos. A haughty nurse looked at me suspiciously, as if I were disrupting the balance of her tightly managed ship. I wondered what would happen if she discovered the hidden cards, and why I would risk the chance to visit my son by breaking the rules.

This particular day, visitors were already in the room where Steven and I usually met. We were directed to a table off to one side of a large area where the residents ate their meals. A staff member stationed at a desk in the center of the room nodded politely as we began to unpack the tacos and burritos. I had been coming to the hospital three to four times a week, long enough so that, aside from catching "attitude" from a charge nurse now and then, most of the attendants were pleasant. They had become accustomed to my visits, so the food items were not analyzed as much as they were in the beginning. Steven and I were not alone in the room, but we were mostly ignored. I caught his eye and nodded to the bag and he immediately picked up on my unspoken message. With a discreet side eye, Steven quickly stuffed the cards into his waistband. In some inexplicable way, sharing this secret reinforced the bond between us.

Steven asked to use the bathroom, and went to stash the contraband cards between the pages of the lime-green New Testament with the black plastic comb wedged inside the back cover. Two rubber bands held everything in place. He had presented this seemingly innocuous possession several times before, but this time, he explained its significance. Inside was a folded picture of a satellite he found in a magazine. The Bible (and what was hidden between its pages) formed some kind of communication device and "gun." He told me he received information from the satellite image, and the "Bible/comb/*Magic* card gun" contrivance warded off evil spirits. I suspected that the Bible and the comb were items Steven was allowed to carry with him in the hospital. It was evident that my son was using anything he could get his hands on to defend himself against the threats coalescing in his troubled mind.

We did not discuss the smuggled cards that day. Steven focused on his food and we talked about his upcoming court date and whether or not he still wanted to stay at the hospital. He was not as sure as he had been when I first arrived on the island. He thanked me again for the clothes and told me how much he appreciated my visits, insisting that he pay for my rental car for the last two weeks of my stay so I could continue to shop for him. He said he wanted me to experience more of the island before I left. I started to protest, but thought better of it. It was clear that Steven felt empowered by his ability to contribute to my travel, and I could not deny him his dignity.

I wondered how he might accomplish this, since it meant coordinating with his case manager and payee in a relatively short period of time, but he knew exactly how to maneuver within the system. Steven was remarkably adept at self-advocating. For me, it was not about money. I would have spared no expense for the few awkward and painful moments I shared with my son over the course of those five weeks. It was about letting him have some control, and allowing him to offer a little of himself in whatever way he could. This physical gesture was an opportunity for him to express his love; it was a substitute for an emotional connection that was so much more difficult for Steven to experience in the advanced stages of his schizophrenia. In that moment, it was enough.

CHAPTER NINE

Ruins to Runes

The highest and the oldest of all the gods is Odin.

Odin knows many secrets. He gave an eye for wisdom. More than that, for knowledge of runes and power, he sacrificed himself to himself.

He hung on the World Tree, Yggdrasil, hung there for nine nights. His side was pierced by the point of a spear, which wounded him gravely. The winds clutched at him, buffeted his body as it hung. Nothing did he eat for nine days or nine nights. Nothing did he drink.

He was alone there in pain, the light of his life slowly going out.

He was cold, in agony, and on the point of death when his sacrifice bore dark fruit. In the ecstasy of his agony, he looked down and the runes were revealed to him. He knew them and understood them and their power. The rope broke then, and he fell screaming from the tree.

Now, he understood magic. Now the world was his to control. (Neil Gaiman, *Norse Mythology*)[13]

Neil Gaiman's version of what is sometimes referred to as Odin's "crucifixion" in *Norse Mythology* so powerfully resonates with living grief that upon first reading, it slams into the heart like a cannon shot. Gaiman's description encapsulates the suffering and complete annihilation experienced in the depths of profound grief. One might argue that because Odin's suffering is self-inflicted, he initiates his own passion. (Indeed, the archaic Latin form of "passion" originally meant "to suffer.") Still, Odin surrenders to the Mother/s Odyssey in its truest sense—transformation through loss. For those who know what it is to grieve, for those whose hearts have been flayed by the loss of a child, or anyone or anything that is beloved, Gaiman's prose rings true. Even though a Mother/s Odyssey can be thrust upon us without warning (or permission), it resembles Odin's self-imposed ordeal. The Mother/s Odyssey *is* a crucifixion. It is a process punctuated by an agonizing assault on one's dignity, a mortal wound to the soul, and absolute isolation.

Loving a son diagnosed with schizoaffective disorder and coping with the end of our relationship as it once was inspired the idea of the Mother/s Odyssey. Grief is a lifelong companion. The death of any human or animal to whom we are deeply bonded is an eternal wound. Over time, perhaps the pain softens, but the trauma remains. The scar, or brand, or *descansos*, as it were, serves as a memorial.[14] We are permanently changed by profound loss no matter the cause, and our grief events redirect our paths in such a way that it feels as if we walk in perpetual grief.

Obviously, grief encounters cannot be collapsed into a single category; they are deeply personal. For example, a sudden loss is one thing, but death as a result of terminal illness is another. In such cases, "letting go" happens under the double-edged sword of knowledge: the awareness that the end is near, and the bittersweet gift of treasuring each remaining moment. For loved ones of individuals on life-support, the agonizing decision over when to keep hope alive and when to let go must be unspeakable. Add to that the heartbreak of losing a child, and the gravity of the Mother/s Odyssey comes into view.

Since grief is such a subjective human experience, one grief cannot be measured against another. Without first-hand experience, it's impossible to imagine the pain parents or guardians face when a child goes missing, or how traumatic it would be to suspend a search when it is the only hope. What about the terror and isolation when the search is ended—or if no one is looking in the first place? Then, there are parents of soldiers who are Missing in Action—how must they feel? Consider the despair and living grief when missing loved ones become cold cases.

Those who lose someone they love to the prison system bear a unique form of living grief. What of the stifling loss when there is no choice but to surrender a loved one to the consequences of their actions, or the unspeakable pain when the consequences do not fit the crime? The burden must be particularly harsh when a loved one has been wrongly convicted.

Living grief is profoundly isolating, but not unique. Each example has its own ravages and rewards. My loss may not be exactly the same as other grief passages, but I know what it is like to live in perpetual grief. I know despair, frustration, and rage. And I know how it feels to hang on that hook in the Underworld with hope collecting in crimson pools beneath my corpse. While our grief wounds are personal, there are parallels between our stories. This common ground is where empathy leads to acknowledgment and validation. As we saw in the story of Inanna, it was the experience of witnessing without judgement that set restoration in motion. Empathy gives birth to momentum, so that one may return from the pits of hell.

Comfort often comes from those who have traveled a similar path. This is one of the ways religion functions, and why individuals appeal to the gods or patron saints like Mary (Our Lady of Sorrows). These divine souls have endured their own "passion." At times, they are the only solace to be found. They may show up in images, stories, or through those who speak the same language—those who know what it means to be laid bare by despair. Whether one loses a loved one through death or through an abiding absence (physical, emotional, or mental), grief is a trauma—and from trauma, no one escapes unchanged.

Loving someone with a serious psychiatric condition is a specific kind of trauma. Mental illness does not carry the finality of death—at least, not at first. There is no single event that marks the "end," per se. Along my path, I have traded in misguided hopes, the belief that things might be different "this time." I know the seduction of denial and the frustration of powerlessness. The Mother/s Odyssey, for me, oscillates between the eternal bond with my son and complete alienation from him. The grief pendulum carries me from one end to the other—I have hope; I lose hope. In this way, grieving is the "mother" of all odysseys, and she is a "bitch." One does not need to be a woman or a mother to imagine this kind of pain, in the same way that one does not need to be a god to understand crucifixion. Where there is love, there is loss, and the loss of the beloved *is* a brutal crucifixion.

My grief over Steven was like a coin—one side represented the active dynamic in our relationship. Another way to describe it is to say that at "high tide," we were connected. We were on the same page. At low tide, we existed in two different dimensions, like Odysseus and his mother Anticlea. For years mother and son were separated; Odysseus was off on his adventure, and his mother grieved in Ithaca until she could stand it no more. Anticlea's frustration drove her to take an outrageous action: suicide. For almost a decade, I lived in my own Ithaca waiting for Steven to return. I could relate to Anticlea's desperation.

Like Odysseus' mother, I was determined to find a way to reach my son. When I first arrived in Hawai'i, I had no way of knowing that what seemed like paradise would become my Hades. While I was not suicidal like Anticlea, over the years there were times I was convinced I could not bear the pain of my son's illness. Though I did not go to the same extremes, reuniting with Steven required a kind of "death." I had to let go, not only of my past relationship with my son, but my *dream* of how it should be. Like Anticlea and Odysseus in the Underworld, I could speak to my son, but was unable to "touch" (or rather, reach) him. I learned Anticlea's painful lesson: separation from one's child was unbearable, but being close, yet unable to reach them was eternal hell.

In the coin analogy, one side (heads) also represented the outward facing dynamic of loving Steven. It was where I was able to take action. I set out on "quests" to find the things he wanted—superhero t-shirts, *Star Trek* books, *MTG* cards—and I provided them. Often, it seemed I was nothing more than Steven's pipeline to the "real" world. However, my quests diffused some of the tension. Something could be done. There was motion; therefore, emotion could, in some sense, dissipate.

Where there is action, there is potential for paralysis. One might assume paralysis is the opposite of action, the "tails" side of the coin. Not necessarily. "Heads" is also where the *inability* to act creates tension. Obviously, the ability to act is a counterpoint to powerlessness. Yet, when action stalls, pressure rises; emotion turns back on itself, intensifying until it finally demands attention. This is what led to Anticlea's suicide. This pressurized powerlessness becomes self-destructive (sometimes violent) as we make our way on our grief passages.

This pressure caused me to contemplate driving my car into a police station nearly two decades before when my son was questioned without a parent (or attorney) present. I also experienced it when a charge nurse turned me away from my scheduled visit, and again when I could not find Shock Tarts in Walmart. When I am powerless to intervene or to act, the subsequent buildup of energy is hard to contain. This tension needs to be strategically siphoned off in order to relieve the pressure.

If the outward facing "heads" of the grief coin represents the pressurized emotions around action and inaction, then "tails" is an about-face: an emotional vacuum. "Tails" becomes the inward facing aspect of loss: a suffocating void that causes one to gaze into the depths of sorrow. Whereas "heads" is the doing and undoing, "tails" is emptiness and regret. For me, it was the sense that my relationship with Steven was severed. Whether permanent or temporary, the trauma of this severing cut to the bone. In a state of profound grief, I often felt flat, shut-down, or dead inside. Like Sethe, taken to her bed waiting for death in Toni Morrison's *Beloved*, this numbing emotional vacuum can drain away the will to go on.

This, I found, was where guilt and shame resided. When one has in some way contributed to the suffering of someone they love, regret leads to a kind of emotional stasis. Moreover, the shame of failing at the fundamental objective of parenting—to protect children at all costs— was, in my experience, a fast track to self-pity. Grief turned inward, as such, feeds on guilt and shame. We may blame others, or the systems in which we are enmired, but mostly, we blame ourselves. As a result, we may carry our guilt and shame like a cross into every situation, looking to exorcise it through self-destructive behaviors that bring about the punishment we feel we deserve, enacting our own crucifixion.

The Mother/s Odyssey and crucifixion are parallel journeys of descent and return. For Odin and Jesus, crucifixion led to renewal. Crucifixion is a descent (similar to Inanna's ordeal), which breaks one down, strips one bare, and causes one to face ultimate death. Odin endured his passion for the sake of divine knowledge (the runes). Whereas his self-sacrifice results in knowledge and power, Jesus sacrifices himself to the will of God, becoming the "messiah," or anointed one.

Their stories have different origins and outcomes, but the implications are the same: something has been lost and something has been gained. One sacrifices divine power for divine knowledge. The other sacrifices his life to reestablish a relationship between humanity and divinity. However, Odin and Jesus come to their crucifixions by *choice*; this is what differentiates crucifixion from the Mother/s Odyssey.

The Mother/s Odyssey, by contrast, is not a choice; it is a result of the loss or the suffering of someone we love deeply, and our inability to intervene. Anticlea's Mother/s Odyssey began in the absence of her son. Mary, as a passive bystander to Jesus' torture and death, was initiated into her own Underworld experience. One could argue that she "chose" her Mother/s Odyssey when she welcomed the divine proclamation that she would bear the son of God. But bear in mind, she was not asked—she was told—she was at the mercy of the divine. Once transformed, her status as archetypal mother, Our Lady of Sorrows, symbolizes the hard-won wisdom of living grief.

Although the Mother/s Odyssey feels all-consuming, one does not have to be consumed by grief. In fact, stages of living grief are much like the perpetual waxing and waning of the moon. The Mother/s Odyssey is defined by cycles of heartbreak, surrender, waiting, and revelation. However, unlike each moon phase, which has a beginning and end, the stages of a Mother/s Odyssey may be concurrent. With every heartbreak, revelation may unfold. Bliss can become an unlikely byproduct in the tension of waiting. Or one might find a kind of mad joy at the point of surrender. This is not surrender in defeat, but in faith, where waiting becomes holding vigil—and surrender, a sacred rite. My journey has taught me this: Where there is revelation, there is a simultaneous rending of the heart.

Can we acclimate to the rhythms of living grief? The truth is, we relearn the same painful lessons time and time again. My journey to Oahu was a reminder. Like Anticlea and Mary, my grief passage was initiated by my son; and it was defined, in part, by cycles of severing and salvaging our relationship. However, the Mother/s Odyssey is not just for mothers. It is part of the human experience, and myths and stories about living grief make meaning out of the misery.

Even though myths and stories are hardly meant to be taken literally, they do have something to say about grief. When Odin sacrificed himself to gain knowledge (knowledge he would eventually share with mortals), his isolation, perseverance, and surrender yielded wisdom. In the mythic tale, he hung upside down from one of Yggdrasil's branches above the Well of Urd. He took his spear and pierced it into his side, but not before commanding the gods not to intervene. He told them not to bring him even one sip of water. For nine days, Odin cried out in pain, until nearing death, he received the runes.[15]

The myth of Odin implies a link between ritual suffering and revelation. The god fully surrenders to the process. Living grief means engaging in the intimate relationship between suffering and transformation. It makes a sacrament of surrender, and wisdom is the bittersweet reward. Those in the process of their own grief passages may apply these principles to their own experience.

Gaiman takes suffering one step further, capturing an oddly sensual quality to surrender, describing Odin's final moments on the World Tree:

"In the ecstasy of his agony, he looked down and the runes were revealed to him." Here, the author exposes the ecstatic potential in suffering—a bliss, or mad joy wildly counterintuitive to pain and powerlessness. Women sometimes report simultaneous ecstasy and agony during labor. This phenomenon may also result from a serious injury or near-death experience. Some individuals describe a moment of "release," a kind of otherworldly clarity and peace.

With this in mind, Mary's serene expression in depictions of the pietà made a bit more sense. Consider Michelangelo's "story" illustrated by *The Pietà* (after all, art is a form of storytelling) alongside Bernini's marble sculpture, *The Ecstasy of Saint Teresa*. In Bernini's statue, Teresa swoons beneath the point of an angel's spear.[16] Her blissful expression is indisputable, and scholars speculate about the sensuality in this iconic piece. The insinuation of pleasure where there is pain is controversial. However, there seems to be a connection between surrender and serenity, and sometimes even ecstasy.

The passion of Christ, Odin's crucifixion, and the Mother/s Odyssey, suggest that surrender is a necessary part of transformation. Our Lady of Sorrows supports that theme—Mary's wounded heart becomes the catalyst for her eternal wisdom and compassion. By her wounds, she is transformed. Therefore, she is content to bear the seven swords in perpetuity.

Swords, spears, and the wounds they inflict are common motifs related to the descent. In stories and legends, to be pierced by a sword or a spear carries mythic import; it emphasizes the link between wound and revelation. In many cases, these wounds symbolize a loss of dignity, consciousness, and control. At the point of wounding, at the point of annihilation, there is no will; the only option is surrender.

Odin, like Jesus, hung suspended between life and death. Both were crucified in isolation, this was something they had to face alone.[17] Like Inanna, they were stripped of their dignity and identity. All three were pierced in some way, their wounds symbolic of the shattering of self as the "ego" dies. Each experienced transformation as a result of unspeakable suffering, and each was renewed.

If living grief is a kind of crucifixion, these patterns promise relief and purpose. The stories point to the potential for transformation. When "Christ," for example, is understood as a symbol for transformation—if "Christ" can be interpreted as an *event*, he becomes the continual restoration (or re-storying) that human beings can also attain.

I tried to hold onto this hope in the midst of the agonizing weeks in Hawai'i. However, when one is in the course of a Mother/s Odyssey, there are times when the only option is to surrender, to wait, and to accept what is. I wasn't convinced there would be any resurrection or renewal for me. All I knew was that I had never felt so alone, or exposed, or powerless.

Odin and Christ (and many other gods and goddesses like Inanna), chart a course through suffering and surrender. There is something eternal about their stories. Their longevity and the patterns in play captivate the imagination. Though many myths and stories are thought of as little more than fantasy, others are regarded as holy, providing comfort and guidance in times of need. We tend to believe that the myths and stories we learn about in childhood, those considered part of one's culture and religion, are "true" or sacred, regarding those outside of our experience as nothing more than intriguing and mystifying fictions. It is common to seek comfort in what is familiar. Living grief, however, strips away all comfort, and we are forced to reevaluate everything we have taken for granted, everything we believed to be true.

If a Mother/s Odyssey is nothing less than crucifixion, and crucifixion indicates transformation, then what is the promise of living grief? The stories of Jesus and Odin, are finite; their suffering ends. Odin falls from the tree and retrieves the runes, and the world becomes "his to control"; Jesus dies and is resurrected, ultimately reigning in heaven. This is where the parallels between crucifixion and the Mother/s Odyssey break down. Jesus and Odin are not crucified again and again. Even Mary, the icon of all grieving mothers, is eventually relieved by her son's transfiguration. She bears witness to his pain *and* his victory. Though she carries the scars of a wounded heart, her son's suffering is over, and it results in something greater for both of them.

For me, the image of Our Lady of Sorrows is especially compelling, because the seven swords protruding from Mary's heart suggest something else—the perpetual path of living grief, or a Mother/s Odyssey. I must admit my aversion to the grotesque agony and ominous lure of this path. It's understandable to want to avoid the intense and disturbing elements of mothering: birth, surrender, death, and grief. Stories and rituals dedicated to these visceral human experiences are often sanitized or suppressed. They symbolize the gut-wrenching, bloody labor of grief, as well the calm surrender to what is. The image of Our Lady of Sorrows is a remnant, a testament to the bliss and brutality of the Mother/s Odyssey.

Since one does not need to be a mother to experience profound grief or powerlessness, it may be helpful to remember that "Mother" also suggests something primary or original. As such, the "Mother" Odyssey becomes a fundamental (even primal) process. Many will make this descent, often more than once. Living grief takes many forms throughout the course of one's life. However, what has been revealed in the ancient myth of Odin is that the "runes" are the prize. What does this mean? Our "runes" offer a new understanding of ourselves and the world, an enduring compassion for the pain others experience, and wisdom gained in the process.

Runes indicate language (historically, they are the Scandinavian alphabet in its earliest form); but they also signify divine wisdom. Thus, Odin's sacrifice yields communication. He shares his knowledge with mortals in order to enter into a relationship, to experience companionship. Only in the relationship to another does compassion exist. The divine knowledge represented by the runes establishes a connection between humanity and divinity. A common language is spoken, and wisdom is exchanged.

This is why Sarah was able to step into my life for a few short weeks during my stay on the island, comforting me in a way that no one else could. She had been on her own Mother/s Odyssey and returned with the runes; we spoke the same language. This is also why I was able to hear her story about the death of her daughter and "get it," to bear witness to her suffering without flinching—neither of us was afraid to stare into that dark, ugly abyss. I could receive her divine wisdom and share my own. For those who understand living grief, the runes symbolize this common language and divine knowledge, and they also speak to our ability to walk alongside those who grieve, to offer healing to their lacerated hearts with knowing silence, and to hold vigil while they cry, or sleep, or sometimes scream.

It is hard to describe the isolation one encounters during some of the more intense phases of the Mother/s Odyssey. Living grief is like being suspended on a high wire over a chasm of despair. On one side, "normal" life awaits, on the other, nothing will ever be the same. Everything about surrendering to this process seems wrong, and yet the stories speak the truth. My life-long Mother/s Odyssey was a tandem journey with my son. In 2018, it was distilled into an intense crucifixion. So, I wrote through my pain, and carried the runes back home.

CHAPTER TEN

Pilgrimage

If runes represent divine knowledge, with that knowledge comes an encounter with the sublime. My last day on the island became both an exodus and a pilgrimage. Those several weeks had been no vacation. Rather, this had been one of the most difficult experiences of my life. I was more than ready to return home; but I did not want to abandon my son. How could I leave him behind, locked in a psych ward? I had been on emotional overload since I arrived, and now it was time to pack all of those emotions in my carry-on and head back to the mainland.

Since I mostly kept to myself during the month-long program at the university, an unlikely turn of events resulted in spending my final hours on the island with a companion. Savannah was a classmate with whom I shared a lunch or two. We arranged to spend our final day exploring Hawai'i, marking the completion of the summer institute, and preparing for the long journey home.

Savannah's bucket-list mission was to swim in the ocean. So, we headed out early, driving along the Windward Coast. I planned to have lunch with Steven that afternoon, and also wanted to locate a church I found online named "Our Lady of Sorrows." My flight was scheduled at 9:00 pm, so we had plenty of time. It was a breezy day and a beautiful drive; the volatile surf and majestic views along the coast were exhilarating. Surfers reveled in the turbulent waves, and further inland, steep walls of a dormant volcano stretched upwards, forming a tropical, natural coliseum. Once we broke away from the mecca of consumerism along Waikiki Beach, it was easy to see the island's appeal. As the Honolulu traffic faded in the rear-view mirror, one might say, Oahu "relaxed," and one could sense a certain gentle ease. In fact, I was so accustomed to the frenetic brusqueness of the Boston metroplex, that there was a noticeable culture shock upon landing in Hawai'i. No one was in a hurry, and impatience felt like a cultural *faux pas*. More than once, I caught myself biting my tongue to keep from snapping at a nonchalant server, but things moved at a snail's pace on "island time," and this was a constant aggravation. After relocating from the lazy pace of a small Midwestern town, it had taken years for me to acclimate to the sharp edgy rat race of Boston. Now, I was the one who had to slow down.

After some time at the beach, Savannah dropped me off at the hospital. There was nothing particularly remarkable about my final visit with Steven until a young nurse asked if I would like her to take a picture of the two of us. This was a surprise. For five weeks, the rules had been very clear about cell phones. Mine was secured in a cabinet in the vestibule as was customary. The nurse finagled permission and hustled me along the corridor to retrieve my phone. She explained that she would hold it and take the picture, returning it to the locked cabinet when we were finished. She also suggested that we go to the "courtyard" to take the photo, because no pictures were allowed inside the facility. To experience the open air for a few seconds with my son was an exceptional gift.

I was a little embarrassed, because I accidentally left the sweater I always wore packed in my carry-on bag at the dorm. Without the sweater, technically I was inappropriately dressed for the hospital. The temperature on the unit was usually ice cold, but I was also mindful of the instructions by the guard on my first visit. Women were asked to cover themselves, so they wouldn't "instigate" the residents on the men's wards. I had been dressed for the beach, and all I had to cover my arms was the travel blanket I used while sitting in the sand. I swiped it from JetBlue on my flight from LAX. Cursing my poor planning, I tried not to think about the fact that in this rare photo of me and my son, I would be swaddled in airplane schwag.

However, I did not have time to be self-conscious; things happened quickly. I sensed some conflict among staff members over this escapade, so I kept quiet and followed instructions. Steven and I posed under a naked basketball hoop affixed to a ten-foot cement barrier surrounding the exercise yard. Draped in my JetBlue shawl, I stood arm in arm with my son as a Jurassic-looking mountain range loomed over the imposing gray wall of the institution.

It had been six years since Steven and I were in a photo together. It was in 2012, when I came to see his new apartment in Eureka, California.

We visited the Redwoods and sipped coffee while staring out at Humboldt Bay. Within a year he was off again, with only a few bucks in his pocket and a one-way ticket to Honolulu. Yet, here I was, reunited with my son, and for one split second it felt real—well, almost. A photo, at least, would make it feel less like a dream. What appeared to be an ordinary act by a shy nurse's aide, was an extraordinary gesture of compassion. I had come so far to reconnect with my son, but much of my time with him seemed only to reinforce the distance between us. This photo would commemorate our reunion and remind me that this surreal dream actually happened.

I thought again about Odysseus and his mother, wondering how she would have felt if she had been able to touch Odysseus in Hades. I think she would have felt as I did. The sun warmed our faces (though it was filtered through a canopy of black net), and the breeze was a glorious relief from the stale institutional air. That simple shift made those ninety seconds feel somehow sacred. I fought back tears, and I thanked Steven's nurse repeatedly. She was an angel; again, thank you Angel.

The compassion displayed in that moment would be one of many encounters with the divine that day. I walked away from my last visit feeling unsteady and raw. Savannah offered to drive to the church I wanted to find. She too was an angel, intuiting when not to ask questions, and when to offer a quiet distraction. I was numbed by the reality that I would be leaving my son in a few hours, and tried to remember, how had I done it before? How had I managed to cope with the physical separation? How could I let go of this moment? How would I be able to return to the land of the living after my Underworld ordeal?

Living grief was a shapeshifter. My Odyssey with a capital "O," encompassed *all* the moments of loving and losing my son—all of the mini-odysseys within the Mother/s Odyssey. Each tiny revelation took me from one way of seeing to the next. Each stage required letting go of one thing to gain something new, to retrieve another rune. My journey to Hawai'i was one of those mini-odysseys. Even though it seemed monumental at the time, it was confined to five weeks. There was a beginning and an end. Those five weeks were a deep dive into living grief, one that allowed me to find a way to tell this story.

The time I spent with my son on the island, however, exposed a new level of grief. This grief was worlds away from those years of anguish brought on by separation, not knowing, and waiting. Hawai'i would forever be my Hades: a journey into my own Underworld where I was able to intersect briefly with my son. Steven was on his own epic adventure, much like Odysseus, and like Anticlea, I could "see" my son but not "touch" him. I could also see how Anticlea's torment in Hades defined her Mother/s Odyssey. She was cursed in eternal exile, never witnessing her son's return to Ithaca, but I was not to remain.

Perhaps, it was the parallels I was exploring between Anticlea and Mary that drew me to an average-looking church named "Our Lady of Sorrows." Hunting down this nondescript chapel became a kind of pilgrimage. Anticlea and Mary were my touchstones; they were reminders that others had endured the Mother/s Odyssey. I felt compelled to pay my respects to Our Lady of Sorrows. In my online search for gallery images of the sanctuary, I found one of a brilliant blue stained glass window with a depiction of the pietà, one of images that kept whispering to me. I needed to see it for myself.

Dark clouds collected in the mountains, as they so often did in the afternoons on the island. Savannah reminded me to look for rainbows while she kept her eyes on the road. We had been schooled on the daily rainbow phenomenon at the university, hearing about the frequent afternoon rains and the rainbows that were a legendary part of the institution's identity. I never saw them while I was there, even though my dorm room had a perfect view of the valley. I looked up at the brooding clouds skeptically. Would it be some kind of sign if a rainbow appeared over Our Lady of Sorrows?

It was Saturday—the place was deserted as we scouted the church grounds. An ordinary-looking sign greeted us with the name of the parish and the worship schedule. Situated in a protected, elongated cubicle off to one side was an open-air sanctuary. For praying in the rain, perhaps? Faded artificial flowers framed a weathered poster of Christ discreetly hanging inside the prayer shack; two rows of plastic lawn chairs faced a clear acrylic wall separating the shack from an indoor auditorium. I smirked at the bizarre caricature of Jesus with pastel laser beams streaming out of his chest like some rainbow gone wrong. Was this my sign? The Savior's right hand was lifted in the iconic Catholic blessing, and thick, white text across the bottom of the poster read: "Jesus, I trust in you!" Peering through the milky acrylic wall into the dim sanctuary, I was reminded of the plexiglass at the hospital, only there were no bars, no steel mesh—no carbon steel drywall screws set off in pairs, staring at me like eyes—eyes filled with blame. But there was pastel Jesus and the artificial flowers; what a great name for a band, I mused to myself.

My sacred pilgrimage felt desecrated. I knew it was foolish to expect something magical might transpire if I made the trek to Our Lady of Sorrows. Still, I was hoping for some kind of reassurance. Since I couldn't see the stained glass from the prayer shack, I followed a sidewalk around the side of the sanctuary where all that was visible was the backside of the window. From there, it was just a crude outline, a patchwork of white mastic and glass segments. Defeated, I made a beeline for the car, but Savannah encouraged me to take more time. We walked around to the front of the church and peaked in a narrow window flanking the front door. I could make out most of the stained glass pietà several yards away. Since the church was locked, a closer view was not possible, but I was gratified that at least I laid eyes on it. It began to mist, prompting me to check the sky once more. Sun rays streamed through clouds, and the air was thick; the conditions were right—but no rainbow.

As Savannah turned the car around in the parking lot, she caught sight of a statue in an adjacent garden. I went to investigate and found an alabaster depiction of the Pietà. I stared at the lifeless body of Jesus draped across Mary's lap; his head was cradled in the crook of her neck. The impressive statue was the luminous focal point in a circle of stepping stones. I saw the flat white stones were cleverly arranged to fashion a rosary. Looking into Mary's peaceful face, the presence of the grieving mother brought about a moment of earnest recognition. Over ten years earlier, Diana Eck (one of my professors at the time) explained this phenomenon; quoting from her book, she described *"darśan"* as seeing and being seen by the divine.[18] This is why icons matter, why human beings need them, and why we embark on pilgrimages to find them. In that moment, I remembered—*darśan* was an encounter with an icon, a moment when the resonance between their story and ours was deeply felt.

A pilgrimage is a journey. Sometimes a journey takes a pilgrim to a sacred place, and sometimes the journey is what makes it sacred. One might describe a holy site as an intersection between dimensions, between earthly and heavenly realms. These intersections are one of the places where divinity can be accessed, where we receive the runes. Stories about these places are at the heart of all religious traditions and, in many of those traditions, altars were built and statues were erected to mark where such encounters took place. One can sense the reverence in these places—a collective acknowledgement, as it were. These spaces are infused with emotion, evoking (and perhaps invoking) holiness, intention, or at the very least, respect.

I have had many teachers—grief is the "mother" of them all. This phase of the Mother/s Odyssey, my pilgrimage to Hawai'i, was a reminder of all I had learned from living grief. It condensed years of loss, including all of the pain that was involuntary, as well as the suffering that was within my control, into a brief, life-altering encounter. Meeting with my son in the hospital (in Hades, so to speak), took me to uncharted depths. It forced me to contend with the *real* loss and accept that the distance between me and my son was not about geography. Not only was I required to release him into his own experience, I was required to accept that I would be ever grieving, ever learning to relinquish the fantasy version of his life, and my unrealistic expectations for both of us. I too could surrender; I could bear my wounds with grace and resolve just like Our Lady of Sorrows. In her enduring serenity she was my teacher, sharing her story, and bearing witness to my living grief.

There was a sad distinction between Anticlea and Mary, and perhaps a lesson as well. Crazed with grief, Anticlea insisted on taking matters into her own hands, ending her life. What might be considered an empowered act was actually suicide—a death sentence. Separated from her loved ones, Anticlea was condemned to Hades to suffer for eternity. Her desire to end her pain only made it worse. I reflected on all the ways I had tried to control my grief, the wasted emotional energy, and how my efforts did nothing but drain the life out of me. This, like Anticlea's path, led straight to the eternal torment of self-martyrdom.

By contrast, for Our Lady of Sorrows, acceptance was the key to her resilience. Mary's legacy was the alternative to martyrdom. She was not static or impassive, she was engaged in active surrender. Bearing the seven swords, she reflected the reality of living grief, and her tranquil expression held the secret. Surrender was grace, and through grace Mary transcended her suffering, which enabled her to provide the same for others. By and large, she had become a vision of tranquility and benevolence. And there she was, dispensing curbside comfort in the mountains of Hawai'i—Our Lady of Sorrows, the archetype of suffering and surrender.

Was this unassuming little church a sacred site on the side of the road, or was my own Mother/s Odyssey what made it sacred? It didn't matter. More than likely, it was both. Ultimately, that which is sacred comes from within—another paradox. As I looked into Mary's eyes, I placed my living grief there on the altar of empathy. I took a breath and took in the sky. Still, no rainbow. But Mary was there; I saw her, and she saw me.

Savannah and I made our way back to the university and I dropped her off at the dorm. Moments later, I was pulled over at a shabby gas station, using a coin-operated shop vac to clean the sand out of the rental car. Out of the corner of my eye, I caught a full rainbow spanning the mountains over the university. It stood out brilliantly, the brightest I had ever seen. The blazing ribbon was pinned behind a lattice of power lines and utility poles. Encounters with the divine can be holy and hilarious, as if the gods have a sense of humor. The message, I suppose, is not to take ourselves too seriously. One may pray to a god from a plastic chair in a prayer shack, or maybe God's artwork is overlaid by power lines; but that is just to say that the sacred is present in the everyday. An hour later on the shuttle to the airport, two more rainbows appeared in the late afternoon sky. I was finally able to exhale. It was time to go home.

CHAPTER ELEVEN

Return

I returned from Hawai'i feeling emotionally battered. All of the coping mechanisms I had used for over a decade, especially those I developed when Steven unexpectedly left the mainland, had to be reconfigured. Observing my son in such a dissociated state was almost more than I could bear. I had learned to live with his absence by developing a kind of fragile acceptance. For the first few years, I would resist, suffer, and lament, repeatedly cycling through the same tired circuit. Over time, I became numb to the ups and downs of Steven's schizoaffective disorder, and the patterns of rejection and reunion. Then, there was the waiting—and heartbreak. The jagged edges of my heart took a beating, like stones on a coastline tumbled by the surf until rounded and smooth. Like those stones, my heart could tell stories for ages. The "smoothness" took the edge off of Steven's diagnosis—from a distance, that is. Proximity, however, changed everything. Seeing my son in May and June of 2018 produced an emotional storm surge, obliterating the polished edges of my heart. Shards reappeared, and the cycle began again.

Once I returned to Massachusetts, it took the remaining weeks of the summer to recalibrate—to regain control over my emotions, and find a way to reenter daily life without feeling like I would dissolve. Silence, nature, writing, and nourishing relationships were my "medicine," slowly allowing me to decompress. But as the semester approached, the pace quickened, and my mind became occupied with lesson plans and scheduling. Around that time, I received a call from Steven saying he was soon going to be released into a boarding house. He sounded excited, but I was cautious. Every moment of Steven's life in Hawai'i had been monitored for over a year. I simply could not imagine how he would be able to transition into life on the "outside" without a tremendous amount of support.

It was Thursday during my first week of classes when he called from a public phone to report he was rooming at a boarding house. I detected the signs of mania in his voice as he told me of his plan to walk to the mall to buy a cell phone. Steven had been ordered to appear at a day-treatment program in Honolulu the following Monday. He would have to take a bus nine miles to get to the facility that morning. If he did not arrive, a bench warrant would be issued for his arrest. Those were the terms of his release.

According to Steven, his case worker was scheduled to bring him money the next day (Friday); maybe he did, but there was no way to be sure. I was sure of one thing—the likelihood my son would make his way to Honolulu Monday morning was slim to none. I was skeptical that any measurable support would be available at the end of the week on a Friday. Steven was heading into the weekend with little resources, an empty room with a bed, and all the freedom he had been deprived of for over a year. I asked him to check in with me the next day; he never did. Throughout the weekend, I repeatedly called the number on my caller ID. A few days later someone answered saying they had not seen him. It was simply a boarding house, and since no one was "in charge," there was nothing I could do. Steven was back on the street.

This was familiar territory. However, less that twelve weeks off of the emotional carousel of Hawai'i, I found it difficult to contain my feelings. I was enraged by what I considered to be a "set up" for Steven's failure. How did any of this make any sense? It was frustrating to think he would no doubt lose all his possessions, *again*. I could not help but fume about everything I had been through trying to locate his endless requests only weeks before, and how all my efforts had been in vain. My frustration was a cover for deeper fears. The hamster wheel in my brain started spinning—how long would it be this time before he surfaced? Would a police officer (or a civilian) see Steven as a threat and shoot him? Would I ever see my son again? Was this going to be the time when I had to let go completely?

I thought about the last time I saw my son before my stay in Hawai'i, during my visit to Eureka in 2012, when we spent a few days together outfitting his new apartment. I bought some curtains for his windows, and we went to a local thrift store to pick out a few kitchen essentials. Steven was in prime form: charming, witty, and inquisitive. He wore a grey long-sleeved t-shirt with "American Rebel" across the front, and confidently sported a charcoal fedora. A cigarette casually smoldered between his fingers as he gestured passionately about his plans to change the world.

We assembled a tool kit for a bicycle Steven used for trips to the store, so he could keep himself stocked with groceries and cigarettes. He prepared dinner in an electric skillet he bought at Walmart, while I hung the curtains. Afterwards, Steven sang and played songs he wrote on a guitar I had shipped to him a few months earlier. I could not help but appreciate his love for performing, as well as his charisma. Steven's songs soared with defiance and desperation, weaving together wisdom and naiveté. Listening to him in that moment, I once again dared to dream that maybe he could build a "normal" life. But before the year was out, my son was off the grid, again.

It is hard to accept that Steven sometimes prefers homelessness. At one point, after being placed in a shelter by the Honolulu county court, he complained that he was not allowed to sleep outside. I wondered about the conditions in these shelters, and if that was what drove him to the streets. Yet, I knew the open air somehow called to my son; it always had. As a boy, he would often devise plans to "camp out" or "live off the land," which seemed to explain those sleepless nights when, as a toddler, he resisted sleeping in his bed (or sleeping at all). For Steven, sleeping in the same place was stifling, and he did not want to be confined. How ironic that he'd spend so much time in custody, and that he would find safety in that. He was seeking an alternative kind of freedom. However, if I let it, his "freedom" could easily become my prison.

For example, when he landed on Oahu in the fall of 2012, Steven called once—then, it was "radio silence" for months. All of my calls went straight to voicemail. Still, I continued to pay his cell phone bill on the off-chance he would contact me. Each month, I scanned the online statement for clues to his whereabouts. That cell phone was the only tie to my son—it was my lifeline. Letting it go felt like abandonment. At one point, someone I did not recognize answered one of my calls. Whoever it was did not seem to know Steven, and I surmised it was likely that he sold it or traded it for drugs or food, or perhaps he got "rolled" again, which was fairly routine. I held on a little longer, but after several months with no evidence of call activity, with a heavy heart, I reluctantly discontinued service.

During the holidays that year, I was living two separate lives. I attempted to balance day-to-day responsibilities of teaching at the college with my grad school coursework. I was also trying to offer emotional support to Devin and Travis in their new roles as fathers, and spend what little time I had with my grandsons. Keeping grief in check was essential; I could not succumb to despair wondering if Steven was suffering somewhere on the streets of Honolulu. Most of the energy involved in living grief—the fear, rage, helplessness, and sorrow—I channeled into my daily activities, which kept me distracted. I immersed myself in hustling the next teaching gig, prepping for classes, and meeting deadlines. Birthdays and holidays came and went. The flurry of life was better than the agony of not knowing if Steven was okay—if he was lonely, hurt, frightened—or dead.

It takes a lifetime to untangle the web of emotion, self-harm, and perseverance woven throughout a Mother/s Odyssey. When one descends into grief, there are options: shutdown (physically, mentally, or emotionally), or throw your shoulder into the everyday routines and plow through. Oddly, plowing through can be just another way to shut down. It might work for a while, and one can accomplish a lot, but the underlying sorrow creates a sense of isolation that makes relationships challenging to sustain. And we lose ourselves along the way. A third option—integrating grief into the day-to-day—takes a different kind of focus; for the most part, it is a slow and painful process.

For years, I could not comprehend what integration meant. Instead, I spent a significant amount of time reacting, hopscotching from one emotion to another, feeling out of control and desperate. This psychic momentum certainly overwhelmed and distracted me from living grief, but the drive to keep moving at any cost, or to plow through, was a cruel mistress. It was an intense and sometimes dangerous energy that fueled self-sabotage. While it was a struggle to find healthy outlets for this powerful force, creativity became a natural channel. Integration happened when I allowed creativity to do its work. It made room for all of my emotions, and gave me a way to make sense of the senseless.

The Mother/s Odyssey amplifies the duality experienced in grief—the need to do, feel, and express, as well as the paralysis, or active resistance. In my case, the momentum of living grief propelled me through a series of milestones, but there was a cost. Though my life seemed to be on track (for there was plenty of doing, feeling, and expressing), another part of me was paralyzed. In fact, this alternate version of me was in a constant state of listening, waiting, and watching for signs of Steven. Paralysis, in this case, was not the lack, but the frustrated abundance of energy—electric, deadly and unpredictable—like lightning. Creativity provided the "ground"; without it, that lightning could wreak untold havoc.

However, when unable to find that ground or direct that energy, the build-up of pressure would become physical. My chest would tighten and ache, as if I were holding my breath too long. Insomnia and nightmares became routine. During the painfully slow overnight hours, I again found myself scanning public records on the internet. Many times, Steven changed his name or used only one name, which made it difficult to track him. During periods of psychosis, he became nonverbal, which explained why he was often detained as "John Doe." Seeing my son referred to as "John Doe" in an official report in a county database was a punch to the gut. Still, whether he was arrested as "John Doe" or "Steven," when he was in custody, at least I would know he wasn't dead.

The longer I went without knowing where Steven was, the more remote and disconnected I felt from the rest of my life. I learned how to compartmentalize the insane worry and despair, because in all honesty, I did not know how else to survive. But at the same time, compartmentalizing felt like betrayal. I was torn, and berated myself for my lack of emotion, as if falling apart was some badge of honor, or martyrdom was a "tribute" to motherhood. Something kept me from emotionally imploding, and I moved through life as if observing from a great distance. If I allowed the tears to come, they might never end; if I began screaming, I might not be able to stop. Even though this time Steven resurfaced within two weeks of his release into the boarding house, his absence triggered the trauma of not knowing whether my son was alive. I felt like a zombie—the walking dead.

In this deadened state, any news was a relief. However, in those few seconds of dread when a voicemail began, "This is (insert name) Hospital," time would stop. I would hold my breath: "Is this it? Is he dead?" The call came that fall in 2018. As the panic subsided and I realized my son had been readmitted, I slowly exhaled. The court had determined weeks before that when Steven was picked up he should be transported directly to the hospital, not jail. Obviously, the judge, the prosecuting attorney, and Steven's public defender realized the "plan" for his release would never work. They acknowledged the seriousness of his condition, but were unable to grasp the complexities of treating and managing schizophrenia. Steven was not a criminal, he was more than a legal problem, he was out of balance—what he needed, they could not provide. So, while the court recognized their approach was ineffective, they fell short of adopting a system that was rational, comprehensive, and proactive.

Ironically, "insanity" appeared to be embedded in the very system that deemed my son mentally incompetent in the first place. Now, charged with making decisions for him, their *modus operandi* was to penalize Steven for *their* ill-advised plan. The entire situation was asinine since my son was obviously unable to comply with the court's directives in the first place. While I was thankful he was returned to the hospital instead of being sent back to jail, I was disgusted that the judge planned for his failure and not his success. Who should be held accountable for "plans" that cost time, money, and staff? Where is the citation or bench warrant for the one responsible for arbitrary decisions resulting in a blatant disregard for those resources? And what about the impact on the victims of this broken system?

Since early 2013, Steven had been institutionalized more days than he had been on his own. Repeatedly, the same judge ordered a panel to determine whether he was fit to stand trial for various offenses from vagrancy to felony theft. The cycle took months, but the pattern was always the same. Pick him up on some kind of charge (most often, a misdemeanor infraction); declare him "incompetent"; hospitalize him and stabilize him on medication; send him to several review panels and court appearances; then, release him without a coherent plan. And the cycle would start again. The process was unapologetically convoluted and irresponsible. At the very least, shouldn't the amount of tax dollars wasted on this bureaucratic juggernaut elicit some kind of investigation into its effectiveness? Squandering the time and energy of an already overburdened support system (doctors, nurses, staff, social workers, and public defenders) was outrageous.

Furthermore, families at their wits' end simply want help for loved ones who are coping with mental health challenges. They have no option but to hope the court will intervene in a positive way. Ignorance and a lack of political will has fueled the dismantling of what limited mental health services there were in the United States. As a result, there are no viable alternatives to incarceration or institutionalization. Neither option provides appropriate treatment. One controls the symptoms through force, the other through medication, but the underlying cause is ignored.

The justice system is no more equipped to handle the complexities of schizophrenia than family members. They are obligated to keep the public safe, but criminalizing mental illness is unproductive, particularly in the case of indigent, nonviolent offenders—not to mention, the waste of public monies. Moreover, managing a severe brain imbalance is difficult enough, but the very institutions which are supposed to provide assistance are a legal labyrinth. Individuals living with severe diagnoses are generally buried in judicial jargon, reduced to case numbers, and become less of a priority as the years pass.

The same institutions, which have little success managing mental health, leave beleaguered loved ones in their wake. Friends and families are powerless. The theme of the grieving mother speaks to their powerlessness too. For example, in the cases of Anticlea and Mary, the gods set things in motion, and to a large degree, they determine the outcome. Today's all-powerful judicial system, in conjunction with the medical system, insurance, and pharmaceutical companies are like the "gods." Arbitrarily, they map out the lives of those attempting to make sense of this unwieldy "System."

Indeed, once the gods put things in play, mere mortals are left to their own devices. What can be learned from Mary and Anticlea about sovereign will, when capricious and high-handed decisions govern one's life? Mary's acceptance was a model for active surrender, but hers was a hard act to follow. However, the result was that she continued on her Mother/s Odyssey, transforming beyond her role as the grieving mother. On the other hand, Anticlea was consumed with her desire to fight the system. She forced the hand of the gods and landed in Hades. There, her Mother/s Odyssey came to a standstill. When Odysseus was sent to Hades to speak with the prophet, he was told to bring a sacrifice to the gods in order to obtain safe passage back to Ithaca. Instead, Odysseus' mother cast herself in the role of sacrificial lamb, sealing her destiny. Anticlea's martyrdom, however, was not necessary in order for Odysseus to find his way; he would have done that anyway. Though she couldn't see it, the gods were providing Odysseus with the resources (and the lessons) he needed to return home. Rather than continuing to evolve in her living grief, or being present to celebrate her son's homecoming, Anticlea remained trapped in her self-appointed hell.

Meanwhile, Odysseus' wife Penelope continued to wait for the return of her husband, but she also set about weaving his burial shroud. Each night Penelope would unravel the threads she had woven that day in order to keep a houseful of greedy suitors at bay. Her act of weaving and unweaving was a poignant metaphor for living grief. Penelope realized that in all likelihood her husband was dead. The shroud symbolized her acceptance of that loss, but the weaving and unraveling illustrated her ambivalence. Even though things looked grim, she did not lose hope. In making and unmaking the shroud, Odysseus' grieving wife was able to balance action with active surrender. This balance offered her what Anticlea forfeited, a "happy ending" to the story; Penelope and Odysseus were reunited at last.

I recognized my idea of a happy ending had to change if I was to fully embrace the Mother/s Odyssey—if I was to accept things as they were, and stop resisting reality. Only then would I be able to appreciate the ways I had been transformed by living grief. If I read the reunion of Penelope and Odysseus as a happy ending (because the lost loved one returned), by comparison, I could feel cheated. Truth be told, Steven might never "return." And while I related to Odysseus' mother trapped in Hades, I did not have to remain—it was my choice. I could choose to sacrifice my health, my wellbeing, and my life; but the outcome would likely be the same. My son's journey would continue without me. Still, the reunion of Penelope and Odysseus was a promise. Maybe the idea of "reunion" indicated something more than the return of Steven, or the restoration of our relationship as it once was. Perhaps, it was the potential for healing and integration.

My grief over my son, in reality, was grieving for myself. Homer's *Odyssey* made it clear that I had returned from the Mother/s Odyssey older and battle-worn, but wiser. Sacrificing myself to intercept Steven's journey was futile. Instead, I could welcome myself home and experience the wholeness symbolized by the reunion of Penelope and Odysseus. With my broken heart in tow, through despair, vulnerability, and madness I had traveled. Now, I was returning to the land of the living. My Underworld ordeal demanded everything I held dear. Although one does not undertake the Mother/s Odyssey by choice, the choices made along the way influence how living grief plays out, and how one endures. We have the option of finding ourselves or losing ourselves. The Mother/s Odyssey is costly—and the price is death.

CHAPTER TWELVE

The Corpse Mother

In a time of mothering, myths and stories can bring hope and perseverance, but they can also inspire dread. Dread is a natural emotion if we are to "die" to any part of ourselves, and a Mother/s Odyssey requires many deaths. Profound loss, for example, is experienced as a kind of death. For those who have been powerless while someone they love is suffering, a part of them dies too. The Mother/s Odyssey is unrelenting, demanding the release of all attachments, making it abundantly clear—the "good mother" must die.

As mentioned before, the "Mother" in Mother/s Odyssey means more than just the one who gives birth, or is guardian to a child. A mythological reading requires that terms like "mother" are seen in their broader contexts. The archetypal mother is the one who protects, cares for, and grieves the loss of another. "Mothering," in its mythic context, can be observed when we look at mothers in myths and stories not only as literal mothers, but as the loving, nurturing, and grieving parts of ourselves. Hence, the work of integration is acknowledging and incorporating *all* of mothering into one's experience: the flawed, indifferent, and destructive aspects, as well as the self-sacrificing, unconditional mother's love that has become the benchmark.

Shame and judgment cast long shadows on mothering; they accompany anything outside the purview of "good mother" territory. Events and emotions, which activate and energize the Mother/s Odyssey, will likely trigger guilt and shame. Further, a severed or broken bond between the mothered and the one who mothers is a trauma—a shock to the psyche. This point of trauma, as observed in the stories covered so far, is the threshold to a tandem descent. One descent is propelled by the other, yet both "travelers" experience the same outcome—disintegration and reintegration. Step one: things are broken down, deconstructed, and dissolved. Step two brings renewal, and the cycle continues. Even so, the Mother/s Odyssey has unique characteristics that are present in many legends and tales of mothers. Aspects of the mother manifest in stories, images, and icons. The good mother (like the quintessential fairy godmother) is one of the most recognizable symbols for life, hope, and renewal. She is the one who intercedes, extends mercy, and offers a soft place to fall. No matter the religion, the good mother appears with her devout followers. Devotees appeal to her aspects of compassion, healing, and long-suffering so that they might manifest those traits in their own lives.

The good mother was present in the stained glass pietà at Our Lady of Sorrows parish in Hawai'i. She was in Sarah's smile, the smile of the broken-hearted finding a way to keep hoping, to keep weaving, to keep breathing. Sarah was one of several emissaries of the good mother who had come to me over the course of my grief passage. These good mothers had experienced a traumatic loss—a child, a faith, a companion, a breast—and each of them embodied ferocious strength and fragility. They followed the emotional currents in their lives, sometimes with calmness, and sometimes with calamity (occasionally with a bit of "crazy"), but always, with courage. The good mother shone through each of them, and their stories soothed my soul wounds. In a blur of tears, I have witnessed these resilient travelers pressing on, under excruciating circumstances. Some have reached out to take my hand, leading the way. Others have met my eyes with an embattled gaze, or a deep, secretive "knowing" that passed between us like a furtive love note, or a flaming torch. The good mother was in these exchanges, expressing compassion and empathy.

The good mother also shows up in a variety of religious depictions—Egyptian goddesses Bast and Isis, as well as the Greek goddess Gaia. Others to be included are Yoruba's Oshun and Yemaya, as well as Buddhist Guanyin, and Mary in Christian traditions. This abbreviated list illustrates that the good mother is the epitome of mercy, compassion, and long-suffering. She is forgiving and kind. Peaceful acceptance is one of her most prominent attributes, and it was earned through blood, sweat, and tears. We appeal to the good mother to show us the way when we are lost. We emulate and aspire to be like her. So what does it mean to say that the good mother must die?

The good mother is balanced by her counterpart: the dark mother.[19]

All aspects of mothering that are less than ideal, unappealing, or revolting are placed on the dark one, who is too often demonized rather than respected. She is all-consuming, the epitome of madness and vengeance, the very image of fury turned back on itself. She embodies murderous rage and devastation. Sabotage, guilt, and depression are also calling cards of the dark mother. She is the death-dealer used to getting her way; and her way is total annihilation. Most prefer to avoid her at all costs. However, like burning the fields before planting a new crop, the dark mother's annihilating presence catalyzes new growth. For those who do the work of mothering, the question is: how does one work *with* annihilation, instead of against it?

The annihilating aspect of the dark mother visited me at various points on my Mother/s Odyssey. I experienced the suffocating despair of helplessness, and I was enraged by injustice. I know well the murderous fury that can be ignited when trying to protect a child, like when I came within seconds of driving my car into a building to "rescue" my son. It is embarrassing to admit that I can be incited to violence, but I can't deny it. Even though I restrained myself from plowing my van into the police station, I know how close I came.

The incredible tension between action and inertia drove me to my breaking point that day—the day my underage son was questioned and arrested without a parent or attorney present. My inability to act was something I could not accept. As my GMC Safari sat idling, aimed at the imposing brick edifice of the station, I felt the escalating pressure as the tension between these two poles was pulled taut—and while the two may be held in balance, once out of balance, all hell breaks loose. Then, the dark mother shows her face.

Consider all of the "acts" of mothering. If a scale were designed to account for these acts, one extreme might be overactive mothering (or smothering)—an abundance of action, which can be just as destructive as neglect. At the other end of the spectrum would be an equally troubling, frustrated ability to act. The pressure of powerlessness elicits all manner of destructive behaviors, perhaps even an abrupt or violent episode like the one we see in *Beloved*. But this is nothing new; myths and stories throughout time suggest mothering can be murderous business. Those who are mothered or who do the work of mothering take heed— mothering may prove lethal.

The ferocity of the dark mother is one side of the equation, but she shows up in those subtle and not-so-subtle patterns of internalized violence too. When we succumb to denial, guilt, and shame, we are in the presence of the dark mother. When despair and isolation lead to self-harm, this is a trademark of the dark one. Her treacherous demeanor represents the annihilation factor. The revulsion she inspires is simply a desire to avoid her unwavering message: *Growth. Means. Something. Must. Die.* Death is fearsome, and the dark mother presses us forward into the abyss where, straining toward transformation (and sometimes struggling against it), we share in her intimate knowledge—what it is to destroy, and to be destroyed.

Traditionally, the "death" of the mother has been seen as a necessary step toward maturity, particularly for men. Sigmund Freud is commonly associated with this idea as a result of his development of the Oedipus Complex, which asserted a boy's wish to replace the father because he wants to possess the mother. Contemporary psychologists (among others) consistently challenged his views.[20] Mircea Eliade, on the other hand, documented evidence to support Freud's belief that the mother is necessarily shunned during transitional phases of a young man's life.[21] Theories about the annihilation of the mother, while no longer widely espoused, have made a lasting impression on the way masculinities and mothering are experienced. As a linchpin of Western psychology, Freud's assertions on the role of the mother still have a noticeable influence on relationships between mothers and sons, and in turn, male/female dynamics.

In the wake of Freud's alleged erasure of the mother, questions are raised regarding the fate of she who is disregarded, silenced, and sometimes eliminated altogether. Perhaps it is only natural that the dark mother should embody the revolting aspects of mothering, for how could anyone separate from the good mother? While the good mother accepts her fate, the dark mother is pissed. Not only does she take on the role of crazed protector, negligent narcissist, or monstrous killer—she embodies the rage of those who have been shoved aside, shoveled under, and suffocated. But the dark mother and the good mother are two sides of the same coin. So, if "mother" is to be more than a placeholder for a child's rite of passage, then what is her role, and how can she evolve?

The stories of Anticlea and Mary indicate that the forsaken mother advances into the grief passage because of a maturing child, a child in crisis, or the loss of a child. These are perfect examples of the literal grieving mother. However, one may be ushered into a Mother/s Odyssey, not by a "child," per se, but by the loss of a connection to a loved one, or another object of one's attachment. In such cases, the tandem descent may not be immediately evident, but it nevertheless exists.

For example: Dennis Patrick Slattery, in *The Wounded Body*, describes a process of making peace with his hip bone the night before surgery, when it would be replaced by a stainless steel and titanium prosthetic. He expresses the profound loss he experienced when his friend, Sister Martha Ann, encouraged him to speak a few final words to his hip. With her help, Slattery was able to release a part of his body, a part that had served him for over fifty years. Acknowledging his grief enabled him to realize: "The wound is a special place, a magical place, even a numinous site, an opening where the self and the world may meet on new terms, perhaps violently, so that we are marked out and off, a territory assigned to us that is new, and which forever shifts our tracing in the world."[22] So it is with grief, no matter the origin.

Certainly, the loss of a hip is not the same as the loss of a child. The point is, Slattery was able to approach his hip replacement from two angles—one was impersonal, all business (in the spirit of the dark mother)—the hip was defective, it had to go—just get it done. And yet, the good mother appeared at his bedside, urging him to acknowledge his *relationship* with his hip. While it must be sacrificed, Sister Martha Ann gave him permission to grieve. Thus, acknowledging the loss facilitated a deeper level of healing, and a hip bone became a catalyst for Slattery's unique Mother/s Odyssey—grieving the body. Moreover, it led him to investigate two transformative questions: "Is being wounded a gift?" and "Is there a gift embedded in the wound?"[23]

Slattery's account demonstrates how aspects of the good mother and the dark mother are interlaced in all manner of grief passages. They exhibit a kind of symbiosis. When we see the good mother and the dark mother as two sides of the same coin, we recognize one of the fundamental principles of the Mother/s Odyssey—and, we can embrace annihilation *and* renewal as part of our grief passage.

So, what can be learned from myths and stories about the grieving mother? To start, whether our children are maturing naturally, taking divergent paths through addiction, brain disorder, or other challenges; whether one has a child or not—in whatever way profound loss manifests—the Mother/s Odyssey is a perpetual cycle of annihilation and renewal. Once it begins, it does not end. It evolves, just as we evolve through it—and, it will likely call us to return, when an occasion arises that requires its unique wisdom.

Annihilation is not only a symbolic or mythic phenomenon; it can be a physical reality. Mircea Eliade pointed to separation from the mother as an accepted part of initiation rituals for young men in tribal communities of Australia. He recognized that when indigenous boys enacted their passage into manhood, for mothers, there was a high price: "mother" became "pariah." Eliade explained that "mother" represented the age of innocence and youthful irresponsibility. Graduating from the realm of the mother meant entering into the realm of maturity. In specific rituals, young boys were violently ripped from the arms of their mothers. Eliade also explored messages embedded in these rituals, which included "aggressive displays" toward the mother signifying the end of child-hood.[24] Myths and stories illustrate the symbolic annihilation of the mother, but the real-world coming of age rituals Eliade studied hinged on literal separation and wounding.

I have often wondered about the unspoken urgency, which pressured my sons to reject mothering as a part of their own coming of age. There were many social and familial expectations—dictates regarding masculinity, in a sense, that made it evident that they had to separate from me. It often felt as if my love, which was at first paramount and sought after, suddenly became a mockery, something disdainful. This was more noticeable in my relationships with Travis and Devin. Steven and I maintained a close bond until schizoaffective disorder made that impossible. During the years when he was lucid, we had several conversations about his experiences with the social pressure to "man up," but he was less influenced by these norms. However, my relationships with Travis and Devin became much more fraught, and they had to contend with the reality that for most of their lives, my time and attention had been focused on their brother. What they couldn't see was that even though I was consumed with crisis management for Steven, I agonized over how they were affected by the unfolding drama in our family. Our brutal emotional separation, and the wounds associated with it, had several contributing factors.

Through these kinds of separations, the mothered and the one who mothers are jettisoned into a new state of being. In stories, transfor-mation is often symbolized by marriage, the fall of an old regime and the beginning of a new, or taking on a different identity. Ceremonies and rituals mark these events. Many times initiates take a new name, or create a new narrative by marking the body. As such, the body (or individual) becomes its own text, according to Slattery, "with a beginning and an end; [. . .] it has a personal myth, an engraving, a marking, a wounding that gives it a particular character and its own unique way of being in the world."[25] Wounds such as these, which signify transformation, as Slattery points out, are "fissures in psyche and soma."[26]

I observed a similar pattern when Steven adopted a new name, a new affect, or radically altered some aspect of his life. At one point, he spent several weeks speaking with an Irish brogue, manifesting a completely new personality. Another time, he refused to use his surname for months; and yet another, he told the court his name was Joseph. I accepted this was a result of his schizophrenia, but I was also aware that he was separating from the identity I had given him. He was becoming his own man, in his own way. Unconsciously, a rite of passage was playing out, seemingly without any corresponding religious or cultural influence.

In American culture, Christianity has played a crucial role in creating markers of maturity, and more specifically, what it means to be a man. Today, ideas about gender are less fixed and increasingly appreciated for their complexity. Still, many cultural rules related to mothering (*especially* what it means to "mother" boys and men) are rooted in archaic soil. Mother/son dynamics and mother/child tandem odysseys (as well as the psychological descent and return they comprise), are mapped by a collection of historical and social factors. Furthermore, the image of Madonna and child sits front and center—she is one of the leading ladies of the idealized mother.

My personal grief passage is rooted in a relatively traditional mother/son relationship, and it is complicated by a variety of influences. However, it bears repeating that "Mother" in Mother/s Odyssey is not exclusive to birth mothers or women, and mother/daughter relation-ships share many of the same challenges, while also carrying their own unique dynamics. Regardless of gender or how one chooses to identify, strong cultural undercurrents impact *ideas* about mothering and how one matures based on history and social conditioning.

Although one of the primary influences on this conditioning in American culture has been Christianity, Freud's psychoanalytic views carry equal weight—and, both hold dubious perspectives on women. In fact, they conspire to arouse reverence on one hand and repudiation on the other, inciting a love/hate relationship with the mother. It is easy to see how the "mother" archetype becomes a lightning rod in this perfect sociological storm.

It was clear to me from my conversations with Steven and my observations of my relationships with Travis and Devin that these influences were (and are) still in play. I watch them continually shape the nature of mothering and the treatment of mothers, toggling between canonizing the good mother and demonizing the bad.[27] These views reinforce polarization, and reduce the world to a series of opposing forces, amplifying exile and annihilation. "Mother" is put on notice— and that is not all.

American pop culture feeds into the notion that "mother" is symbolic for that which must be rejected in order to advance or mature. For decades, there has been a prevailing condescending attitude toward young adults who delay or refuse to leave the "nest." The trope of the socially awkward "slacker" living in mother's basement implies there are rules about becoming an adult, especially for men. Attachment to the mother is seen as a lack of maturity, a sign of weakness, a subject of ridicule. This complicates an already painful dynamic, particularly when the mother/child bond is under tension as a result of separation or estrangement.

Though maturity necessitates the bond with the mother (the prover-bial, albeit literal umbilical cord) naturally must be severed, this loss can be a painful blow even in the best of relationships. Any adult/child who grieves this loss a little too long, or a bit too deeply, is labeled immature, insufficient, or weak. The inability to separate from the mother is a point of contention—a pathology.

An example of this message in pop culture is Alfred Hitchcock's *Psycho*, where Norman Bates continues to live in the oppressive shadow of a literal corpse mother (indeed, a dark mother). Throughout the movie, his childlike adherence to "Mother's" rules, his inability to leave her house, or rid himself of her abusive and domineering presence, stunts Norman's maturity and prevents him from developing relationships. Though she is dead, her corpse reigns over him from the attic. Norman, unable to break from his mother, becomes a psychotic killer. The message is clear—mother must be rejected, or the consequences are dire.

The dark mother has many representations. She takes on the symbolic and sometimes literal role of one confined, condemned, or killed (hence, the "corpse" mother). Not only in mythology, but in folklore and fairytales one can find examples of corpse mothers, sickly, and silenced mothers, as well as suicidal/murderous mothers. These radical portrayals turn any idealized notion of mothering on its head, bringing the dark mother into the light, so she may be fully apprehended.

I began to see myself in the corpse mother, as well as in all of the faces of the dark mother. While on one hand, I might be performing all of the "good" mother tasks for Steven, at the same time I was no doubt the dark mother: neglecting, abandoning, and damaging the emotional needs of Travis and Devin. I felt ever-torn in three separate directions, and eventually time ran out. What had felt like it would never end—the years of rough and tumble boyhood, awkward growing pains, and total immersion in the frenetic day-to-day—was suddenly gone. As my sons became men, the natural progression of separation felt punitive and permanent, perhaps amplified by the unintended fallout from my inexperience (or inability to mother effectively). This separation left me feeling lifeless, and the corpse mother haunted me, stirring up questions about my role now that my sons were becoming men.

In my search for answers, the corpse mother first made herself known in one of the most famous texts in Hindu mythology, the *Mahabharata,* when the Pandava brothers went into hiding in order to avoid being killed by their enemy. Before they adopted their new aliases, Arjuna and his brothers concealed their weapons at the edge of the forest. These weapons (closely tied to their identities as warriors), were set aside, so that their transformation could begin. To mark the tree where the implements were stashed, the men hung the corpse of a woman in its branches. They deemed the corpse their "mother" before they proceeded into a thirteen-year exile, which resulted in the realization of their righteous warrior status. Here, the corpse mother becomes a signpost, heralding the transformation of masculine identity. The corpse mother (the annihilated one) was a symbol of, and sacrifice to, the self-actualization of the brothers.

Similarly, violence against the mother appears in an Egyptian myth about Isis, as a part of a rite of masculine ambition and maturity. Isis's own grief passage was set in motion by her husband's murder. Her brother Set, after killing her husband Osiris, dismembered his corpse and scattered the pieces. Isis collected them, and in her desire to bring her husband back from the dead, she reassembled his corpse, filled his body with her own breath, and conceived a son with him. Afterwards, Osiris was resurrected into his new role as King of the Underworld, and Isis escaped into exile with her son, Horus.

Isis's story continued, and it spoke volumes as I grappled with my identity as mother, and a sense of disorientation and wounding. After many years, Horus avenged his father and secured the throne. Infuriated when Isis extended mercy to his uncle Set (an obvious act of the good mother), the enraged Horus beheaded her. In some versions, Isis remained a headless pillar of stone after retreating to the mountains. Here, rage and grief commingle in the specter of the decapitated mother. Again, the good mother must die. When Horus delivered the mortal wound, he effectively separated himself from his mother; he cut her off without hesitation or regret. In this symbolic act, Horus also severed Isis from her identity as "mother." Thus, a two-pronged assault—the severing of the mother/child bond and the eradication of the former mothering role—suggests that the wounding of the mother is concurrent with the evolution of masculine identity.

The myth goes on: Osiris was resurrected and established as King of the Underworld, and Horus proceeded to reign in Egypt. Yet, Isis too, became immortalized; she was categorically transformed. As the decapitated stone mother, she represented the loss of identity, sanity, and reasoning intrinsic to the Mother/s Odyssey. Yet, in subsequent depictions, the goddess came to be seen with the head of a cow—a sign that she had progressed through her unbearable grief into a new state of being.

The myth of Isis illustrates a phenomenon specific to the Mother/s Odyssey. When the mother/child bond was severed, the mother went into exile. Though Isis *ascended* into the mountains rather than *descending* into the Underworld, she was fully immersed in a grief passage. Eventually, she lost her head. Her decapitation indicates complete annihilation, not to mention humiliation. This annihilation and loss of identity can easily befall the one who mothers, since the expectation for mothers is that they willingly sacrifice themselves for their children—they have no other purpose but to serve their loved ones; they are (stone) pillars of long-suffering and compassion. Always.

Many mothers and other well-meaning individuals came to me offering advice about how to maintain control over my sons, even as my sons were stepping into their own identities as men. They reinforced expectations that the mother bond was fixed, unyielding just like that stone pillar. I, on the other hand, was finding that if resilience was to be found, it was in flexibility. I was having to release my expectations about what mothering meant, and to disentangle myself from the expectations of others.

Expectations drive many who do the work of mothering into unhealthy attachments. The difference between a natural bond and an unhealthy attachment is seen in an over-identification with the role of mothering. I had been resisting the reality that my role was temporary. However, the danger of over-identification was becoming clear: if the relationship does not mature, no one matures. The unhealthy mother, however, must never allow maturity to transpire, because the loss of the mother/child bond would be tantamount to losing oneself or death. No mother wishes to share in the fate of Isis. Her son's act forced the changes that needed to take place, and decapitation (losing one's head) symbolized the loss of the former mother identity, and the coming evolution. In many ways, my sons and I have played out this story again and again. The myth of Isis helps me reframe my frustration as our relationships continually evolve.

Arguably, tales of death and dismemberment indicate something precious is lost. For the one who mothers, grief is like a tidal wave slamming into the shoreline of our existence. Mothering (bringing forth life and/or nurturing) carries a unique intensity that is surprisingly seductive; there is considerable power in being the focus, as well as, the source of love and devotion. Those who have mothered infants and small children recognize this power. It is a force—an energy that makes things right. All of the magical good mother attributes come to the fore: the ability to heal, dry tears, and make monsters vanish. There is a moment in every mother/child relationship, no matter how brief, when "mother" can do no wrong. Once this enormous power has been unleashed, it can be very difficult to redirect. Further upsetting the mother apple cart is the realization that she is no longer in control. That time has passed. The Mother/s Odyssey dictates that control must be relinquished; indeed, something precious will be sacrificed.

Letting go is the primary task of living grief. No longer able to control the outcome, some find themselves forever seeking a new "child" (a stray, an orphan, a pet, an obsession/addiction, or project) in an effort to maintain the status quo. Naturally, this creates all kinds of tension; frustration builds, as growth and maturity stall. Overactive mothering is not relegated to the traditional role—it may extend to romantic partners, friendships, and even professional relationships. One is compelled to "mother" incessantly, because of an inflated view of their role. They cannot help but infantilize, dominate, or smother the other out of a need to maintain control and relevance. The intense emotional energy of mothering run amok is one of the faces of the dark mother, and she is likely to bring about disaster.

Greek mythology is filled with examples of a darker side to mothering. Four sisters from the House of Thebes (Agave, Semele, Ino and Autonoë) demonstrate rage, madness, and despair—all aspects of the dark mother. The Theban sisters were cursed by Dionysus, each tragically losing a son.[28] But the rage and madness associated with the dark mother was exemplified by Agave. Her son, Pentheus, was dismembered after spying on women's rituals during a festival celebration. Under the spell of Dionysus, Agave did not recognize Pentheus, and ripped him limb from limb, when she and the rest of the Maenads mistook him for a lion. In the throes of madness, she triumphantly carried the head of Pentheus back to the king before she realized she had murdered her own son. In her horror and humiliation, Agave went into exile. She was forever cursed, renowned as "most wretched of all mothers."[29]

Semele, the mother of Dionysus (son of Zeus), was known for her untimely demise. Her lover's jealous wife (Hera) tricked the pregnant Semele into insisting that Zeus reveal his true form. Since mortals could not bear the sight of the divine, when she saw her lover in all his glory, she died before giving birth. Zeus, however, took the fetus and sewed it into his thigh in order to bring his son to term. Later in the myth, Dionysus goes to Hades to rescue his mother (not unlike Odysseus). However, Odysseus could not save his mother. He had to leave her behind. Semele, on the other hand, was reunited with Dionysus, and transformed into the goddess Thyone on Mount Olympus. Semele, like Mary, became the immortalized good mother.

Semele's sister (Ino) was truly a "wicked stepmother." She plotted to eliminate her stepchildren by persuading her husband to sacrifice his son. Some suggest her husband was mad, cursed by Hera, and after Ino gave birth to two sons (Learchus and Melicertes), he murdered Learchus. When he came after Melicertes, Ino took her surviving son and threw herself into the sea, drowning them both. In other versions, Ino's husband succeeds in killing Melicertes. Whereupon, Ino (with the corpse in her arms) drowns herself in the waves—now a corpse mother, she is reunited with her son, and the two become sea gods.

Not all of the Theban sisters, however, were as dark as Agave and Ino. Autonoë's story mirrors Mary's, in that she was also unable to prevent the death of her son. While hunting with his hounds, Actaeon saw the naked goddess Artemis swimming nearby. As punishment, the gods turned him into a stag; subsequently, he was ripped apart by his own dogs. Autonoë scoured the countryside looking for her son's body. However, since she did not understand the circumstances behind his disappearance, she was not looking for a stag; she was looking for Actaeon, the young man. Her search was unsuccessful. Overwhelmed and exhausted, Autonoë fell into the deep sleep of despair.

Death, dismemberment, and despair are essential components of the Mother/s Odyssey. They are signs that the descent is in progress. Stories like these suggest that annihilation is a violent process, as well as a precursor to transformation. While obviously, they are not a tutorial for mothering, myths and legends do expose the dark side. When the mother appears, no matter what form she takes, there is no question of her power. But power unchecked leads to suffering and grief. Grief is dark mother energy at critical mass. Even gods and goddesses are unable to escape it. They lament. They rage. They scheme. But they embark on a Mother/s Odyssey, just like the rest of us.

For gods and mortals alike, dark mother energy—the madness, rage, and despair encountered in the grief passage—is nothing short of obliterating. These stories of gods and goddesses expose the volatile emotions present in the Mother/s Odyssey. They illustrate that it is no surprise that mothering is complicated; it can be ugly, dangerous, and agonizing. But they also show that it is natural for mothering to end— mothers mother for a time, and then they evolve, coming into new identities and new roles.

Setting these stories next to my own, I was able to find context for the irrational and violent aspects of myself. Steven's schizoaffective disorder, his erratic behavior, the instability and injustice of it all often drove me to points of irrationality; for instance, holding on to the belief that he could respond and interact with me as he once had. I was so overwhelmed by my inability to meet all of my sons' needs, that I felt as depressed and exhausted as Autonoë, and as desperate as Ino. In isolation and shame, I have often lived in exile, believing that I, like Agave, was a "most wretched" dark mother. But the dark mother is so much more than a "bad" mother.

It is better to cooperate with the dark mother than to resist her, for in the end, she will have her way. She is the source of nonattachment, when we need to be loving but firm. She is the inexhaustible warrior, the shame we carry, the bottom of the barrel, and death. The dark mother is the one who breaks us down, but also the one who picks us up by the scruff of the neck and kicks us back into play. She marches us straight into madness where we are dismembered, decapitated, and destroyed. But we can be assured, *this* corpse mother brings transformation. Stories about the dark mother offer warnings and the wisdom to persevere. They help us connect empathy to the enormity of loss—and once we allow the good mother to die, once we stop hiding from the dark, we can begin to imagine a way forward.

My experience in Hawai'i was a deep dive into grief. I had taken the dive before, but these were new depths. Spiraling downward, the descent of the Mother/s Odyssey drove me squarely into the realm of the dark mother. It was another season of dying, where I was forced to recognize my desire to control Steven's life, as well as, my desire to control my dark mother tendencies. Those extraordinary desires make the tension between action and inertia intolerable. Since much of my time on the island was spent feeling out of control, I know intimately the explosive pressure of that tension. My need to control, however, had to die.

But my dreams had to die too—all the ways I was holding on to mothering, the irrational belief that I could be the good mother and save my sons, or that I could change reality, relive my relationships with Travis and Devin, or reconnect with Steven. Expectations, hopes, magical thinking, and avoidance—all were dying. This was not the first time I had been driven into the realm of the dark mother, and it certainly would not be the last. However, there is no sidestepping annihilation when it comes to living grief. Grief can be so overwhelming, so disorienting, it sometimes becomes "crazy-making." The crazed mother, the broken mother, and the corpse mother—they became my midwives on the Mother/s Odyssey.

Those who know living grief also know the "look" of the crazed mother; we empathize with her. Modern day stories pick up where mythology leaves off—for example, Winona Ryder's portrayal of Joyce in the tv series *Stranger Things*, or Tilda Swinton in the movie *We Need to Talk about Kevin*. These actresses, in complete contrast to one another, "nail" performances of annihilation and dark mother energy. Joyce with her wild-eyed, insane love and relentless ferocity is both alarming and endearing. With bull-dog intensity, she will never let go, in order to save her son.

Swinton's Eva, is the indifferent mother unable to bond with her sociopathic son, raising the ethical dilemma of her responsibility when he becomes a mass-shooter at a nearby high school. Eva is the walking dead, a true corpse mother, broken by guilt and grief. Even so, she channels the dark mother in order to continue loving her son who murdered her husband (who is the representation of the good mother) and their daughter, as well as several students and teachers. These contemporary stories are reflections and refractions of the mother archetype. In "getting it right," they acknowledge and unpack the sufferings of the Mother/s Odyssey for the rest of us.

My suffering was not about my sons, it was about my death—the death of the good mother, the recognition of the dark mother, and a complete release of control. My "wish" for Steven was the source of my grief as I sat with him in the hospital. My inability to comprehend his vagrant lifestyle meant I experienced Steven's desire to "live homeless" as a tragedy, even though his was an entirely different perspective. From his standpoint, my son had determined how he wanted to live and decided that Hawai'i was the best place to achieve his goal. Then, he bought that one-way ticket to his dream—some might consider that admirable. Likely, it was not what he expected; maybe he got more than he bargained for, but Steven was not complaining or begging to leave the island. Occasionally, he entertained coming back to the states, but not seriously. He was living his life. My role was no longer mothering, not in the way I had known it. Yes, my dreams for Steven died, but as a result, they made room for his. My brutal descent brought me to this place, and now, the true grieving could begin. I had to let go, to keep letting go, again and again.

All of the mythical mothers had been here. Mary, Semele, and Isis— they made their return transformed (each of them adopted new identities). Poor Anticlea languished in her personal hell, caught in a destructive loop of trying to control Odysseus' return. As such, she was forever cut off from her son and trapped in her own misery. The stories of Ino and Agave suggested that some journeys are controversial. They speak of the transgressive mother, the one who does not fulfill the good mother role, and her legacy of shame. And while the good mother is ultimately rewarded, the reward is not without great sacrifice. The grief passage sometimes requires her death.

Living grief necessarily reveals all of the facets of ourselves—the good and terrible, and all aspects in between. Like the mythical mothers, we also die to versions of ourselves that are no longer relevant or functional. We may actively embrace this process by cycling into the next phase without resistance; we take on new identities, pass in and out of exile, and integrate rather than ignore each aspect. But, there must be death, and each death is a sacrifice to renewal and a catalyst for maturity (or wisdom).

My story, in conversation with these mythological readings, has expanded my understanding of living grief. The question is: What am I really grieving after all? Is it Steven's diagnosis? Or is it my wish for what his life could be? Is a part of my grief rooted in the inability to have what I want? More importantly, is what I want for my sons what they want at all? I doubt if the essence of grief can ever be completely defined. However, I do know that while the Mother/s Odyssey may be set in motion by death or profound loss, it also requires a willingness to die to oneself.

CHAPTER THIRTEEN

Death Dance

It was springtime a year after my return from the island and Steven's birthday was approaching. Once he was readmitted to the hospital, my son called faithfully every Friday with something he wanted: more *Magic* cards, a book of true stories about the CIA, and another battery-powered radio. He asked if I would replace the Under Armour clothes he lost during his two weeks of freedom. Although it was frustrating to shop for items I worked so hard to find months before, at least now, I understood their significance. And the truth was, it was much easier to shop online than in Ala Moana Mall. I was reluctant to become Steven's personal buyer again, but I knew my son's list of requests gave him something to look forward to—and it was our only way to connect.

Steven called one Friday to tell me the CIA book arrived. When I asked about the radio, I was mildly annoyed when he said he hadn't been using it. Then, he enthusiastically reported that the staff had approved snack packages (all of which must be consumed in one sitting); and he bombarded me with a new set of requests. I felt my blood pressure rise. The logistics of shopping and shipping were a terrible inconvenience with my schedule. Of course, I did not complain—what mother would? But I began to dread the Friday phone calls. Still, I set about selecting snacks my son would enjoy, toting them to the Post Office twice a week.

If I was unable to get Steven's packages in the mail in what felt like a timely manner, I was wracked with guilt knowing he was waiting for them. Even more frustrating, the boxes I managed to mail successfully were most often delayed once they reached the hospital. It seemed "hit or miss" whether my son would receive his care-packages. Online tracking for a pair of shoes Steven asked for showed they had been delivered. Three weeks later, he had not received them. I contacted his social worker, asking if she could help. She said, according to staff, Steven wished to "donate" the shoes to someone else. Steven denied this during our next phone call, and I chalked it up to miscommunication. The next time we spoke, he had his shoes, and I suspected something had gone awry at the hospital.

Around the same time, one of Steven's more unusual requests was a magician's robe. He explained this would help him develop stronger spells of protection. I was skeptical that his CARE team would approve anything resembling a magician's robe, imagining the spectacle as he paced the halls shrouded in black velvet. Steven, of course, assured me it was "fine." There was no way for me to know how the staff felt about my son's progress, and I never received an invitation to attend meetings regarding his treatment (though I offered several times). Common-sense told me they were absolutely not going to permit him to dress like Harry Potter.

So, I considered myself fairly clever when I found a pseudo-robe that was more of a surfer-style hooded caftan for men. It was fashioned out of lightweight, pale green gauze, with the hem falling a little below mid-calf. I thought it just might fly under the radar of the CARE team (it was Hawai'i after all); and I reasoned the look of it would satisfy my son's desire for something "magical." I hoped this would give him a sense of comfort without taking things too far.

A caravan of packages was on its way to the hospital, all set to arrive on or near Steven's birthday: a new book he wanted, the "magician's" robe, $100 in Under Armour apparel, and a care package of specifically requested birthday donuts and candy bars. I ignored the voice in my head telling me I had become Steven's phone order commissary, conflicted about the position in which I found myself, again. Reflecting on the panic I felt in Hawai'i a year before, I noticed that even though fulfilling my son's wish list was stressful, this time was different. My anxiety was on high, but mostly, I was tired and sad.

I decided to include a rare handwritten letter in Steven's birthday card. I wanted to express how much I missed him, and that I remembered. I remembered how close we used to be. I tried to explain that no number of things I could send would fill up the space between us. I assured him that I would always be there, and I would try to provide whatever comfort I could, even if it only came in the form of powdered sugar donuts or a conga line of Fed-Ex packages. I wanted my son to know that I loved him and I was proud of him for always trying, for being a good person, and that I was changed for the better for being his mother. I folded up the letter inside his birthday card, tucked it beside the donuts, and sealed the cardboard mailer.

Steven called a couple of days before his birthday, before the parcels began to arrive. He wanted me to send a set of dice so that he could play a game with his roommate. I felt a recurring disappointment while listening to his latest request and decided to try to bridge the divide. I told him I wanted to support him however I could, but that sending all of these "things" felt like an empty gesture that didn't help anything at all. Suddenly, his whole demeanor changed, and the tone of the conversation shifted. Through thick, labored speech, his words rang clear:

"Mom, don't worry 'bout me. I'm okay. Whenever you wanna worry, you need to think about people in the military who live on ships. It's kinda like that."

I waited for him to continue.

"You know, sailors have rations, and they only eat candy and stuff like that once a week."

"Really?"

"Yeah, I'm doin' pretty good. I've got a bed and three meals a day. It's like living on a ship. So, don't feel bad, okay?"

My heart cracked a little, like an ice cube when first dropped into a glass of water. In his own way, using his specially-colored lens, my son had reimagined his situation for me. Steven was reaching through the veil between us in order to comfort me. Though his was a language of junk food and Navy ships, what he was saying was: "I'm not the one suffering, you are." This connection with my son was a gift after existing in the wasteland for so long. The moment was fleeting, but I felt his presence. Years of distance and despair became instantly absolved by twenty seconds of real communication. I thanked him for sharing his analogy, told him I loved him, and we hung up shortly after.

Two days later, it was Steven's birthday and, since mail was routinely held up at the hospital, I contacted his social worker to let her know he would be receiving gifts. She said she would check with the staff. Moments later she sent a text with apologies saying Steven's CARE team decided all packages would be "returned to sender." I was dumbfounded, and immediately called the hospital asking to speak to someone in charge, something I had not done in years. A man named Richard brusquely responded to my inquiry about Steven's packages, becoming defensive when I questioned his decision to refuse parcels already en route. The social worker assured me it was against policy to withhold resident mail. However, Richard proceeded to tell me that I "knew as well as he did" just how manipulative residents could be, and that he had tried to be accommodating to "this young man," giving Steven "every chance," but he simply would not allow him to "set up shop" at the hospital.

"He is absolutely not going to set up shop here on my watch! You want your son living in the state hospital? Is that what you want?" he barked.

I blinked as I took in his condemnation, then explained that while I didn't like it, I had to consider that the hospital might be the best place for Steven.

"He cannot live here!" He rudely interrupted, talking over me. "We don't have the money or staff for him to set himself up here."

With measured words, I told Richard I was aware how overworked and underpaid he and the rest of the staff were; that I was not trying to make things more difficult. I reminded him, it wasn't my decision that was wasting the hospital's time and money. That was the prerogative of the court, who released Steven too soon without a plan.

"He was *not* released without a plan!" Richard shot back.

Uh oh. That hit a nerve. My hand gripped the cell phone tighter, and I took a deep breath. "Look, Richard. It's Steven's birthday. I just want him to get his birthday card with the letter I wrote. Whatever you decide to do with the packages is up to you. Please understand how frustrating it is that the rules keep changing as to what he can have and what he can't."

Richard's voice rose "*The rules do not keep changing!* I am not going to have you twisting my words. And by the way, did you really think it was a good idea to send him that book on the CIA?"

I was incredulous as he went on to criticize me for sending Steven's *Magic* cards. I was no longer listening; I was trying not to scream, fearful I would make things worse for my son.

"If there are things that you believe Steven shouldn't have, please let me know. Communication would be helpful." I tried to remain calm.

His tone didn't waiver. In fact, he seemed to turn up the sarcasm.

"You are welcome *anytime* to attend our team meetings."

"Oh really?" I replied. "Sign me up! You just let me know when they are, and I'll be there." Now, I was angry.

"Okay, we'll do that." He seemed somewhat put off.

"Great! Please, just make sure Steven gets his birthday card."

"I will."

"Thank you."

I was shaking when he hung up, and immediately, I felt myself split in two: one half was in total combat mode—Richard was about to experience the dark mother! The other smiled and nodded, recognizing this whole scene was like some cosmic "set up." Richard, in his accusation and blame, embodied everything I was learning to release. Unknowingly, he was throwing all of my shame, reactivity, and judgment back in my face—placing the responsibility squarely on me to police Steven's wishes, insinuating my abandonment, and attacking the only way I was able to show love and support to my son.

Of course, I didn't like playing "Santa Claus" to Steven's endless Christmas list, but I understood there was something in my son's desire (and the fulfillment of that desire) that helped him pass his time at the hospital. In waiting for something to arrive, and in coming up with his next wish, he was able to focus on the anticipation. When something arrived, the thrill he received from that fulfilled need was short-lived. So, he had to come up with a new request in order to get his next "fix." Steven was thirty-two-years old, but we were still playing out a psychological mother/child dynamic of "need fulfillment" which was soothing for him. I was doing the only thing I could to connect with my son, whether "Dick" liked it or not.

I called later to wish Steven "Happy Birthday." I listened for signs that he was being "punished" for my phone call, but he was distant and flat. When I asked if he got my card and letter, he said, "Yeah, they let me have the donuts." He was quiet regarding the news about the packages. When I mentioned my offer to attend CARE team meetings, Steven didn't say a word.

I reached out to Steven's social worker immediately following my conversation with Richard, telling her we needed to both be present at the next team meeting, and to let me know when it was scheduled. She did not respond. Steven became increasingly remote, calling less frequently, and when we did speak, he would end the phone call quickly saying, "Well, Mom, I've got some stuff to do, so I'll talk to you later."

Really?

I realized that the latest decree from the powers that be were preventing Steven from succeeding in the need fulfillment game with me—there was no longer any incentive for him to engage. Rather quickly,

I was seduced by the dark mother into a riptide of self-loathing, guilt, and shame. My despair was a byproduct of the never-ending cycle of reunion and rejection that defined my relationship with Steven. If we were able to connect in the smallest of ways for the briefest of moments, I found the strength to go on. I felt validated and rewarded for all of my suffering. Whether I was sneaking contraband *Magic* cards into his unit, "bending" the rules to introduce him to a friend, or disguising a magician's robe as a caftan—when we were able to conspire to "beat the system" it was a "victory," a connection, a shared secret that cemented the bond between us. That was no more. Now, my son needed to find a more productive pipeline to fulfill his needs. I was no longer the available conduit. Once again, the Mother/s Odyssey served up her bitter medicine.

I thought about the Hindu myth about the grieving god, Shiva. In despair over the death of his wife Sati, he carried her corpse around the world lamenting the loss of his bride. Shiva's grief disrupted the cosmic order until another god, Vishnu, intervened. Vishnu secretly followed Shiva and cut pieces off of Sati's body. As each piece landed on the earth, a sacred site—a place of worship and remembrance—came into existence. When nothing was left of Sati's body, Shiva retired to the mountains in peaceful meditation.

Even the god Shiva was unable to *strive* to end his grief. As each piece of his wife's corpse fell to the ground, Shiva had to release Sati a little at a time. In letting go, something sacred manifested. This is one of the realities of my own Mother/s Odyssey—I was constantly letting go of pieces of my relationship with my son. I could only hope that Shiva's meditative retreat to the mountains promised a merciful tranquility I had not yet found.

With each realization, each difficult turn on my passage, a piece of my grief fell away, just as it did for Shiva. This happened, not through my own will, but through grace. The myth suggested that in releasing that which I had been carrying, transformation was possible—an ability to make sense of the senseless, to believe again in something right and beautiful, and allow a hellish loss to become a holy sacrament. Stories gently (and sometimes not so gently) lead me to forgiveness for myself, for my son, and for an inept system that wounded us over the years. Letting go of all of it was the key.

Mary's serene expression was no longer an affront, nor was it a mystery. Actually, it made perfect sense. One did not avoid living grief—one practiced surrender. All of the myths and stories lead to this conclusion: the key to integrating profound grief was in experiencing it fully. Over time, piece by piece, it fell away, giving birth to something sacred. Yes, I would carry the wounds forever—like Our Lady of Sorrows, I would live with the swords in my heart—but that did not mean I was debilitated. Indeed, the swords were the evidence of an incredible battle, but it wasn't me against the world. Nor was it about me protecting my son. It was the internal battle of trying to avoid living grief. Fully experiencing the loss of my son was a loss so profound I thought I would not survive.

My desire to avoid that loss was what drove my ongoing participation in the need fulfillment dance with Steven. It was like the tale of *The Red Shoes*. I had first read Clarissa Pinkola Estés' interpretation of the folktale (in her book *Women Who Run With Wolves*) when he was a boy, noticing it was worlds away from the 19th century Hans Christian Anderson version from my childhood. One thing was the same: each began with the death of the mother, and they ended with the red shoes nearly dancing the young woman who wore them to death. In both cases, dismemberment was the result. In the end, the girl whose feet were fused into the demon shoes appealed to the executioner, and they were mercifully amputated.

My idealized notion of mothering had been dying a slow and painful death over the past two decades—and my journey to Hawai'i instigated a very personal "death" and dismemberment. As in *The Red Shoes*, my role as the compassionate good mother, the nurturing protector, and long-suffering provider—had to die. I became like the orphaned child in the story, vulnerable to the lure of the red shoes. When my role as the good mother was no longer an option, I was lost—eagerly strapping myself into those prized red shoes without understanding the consequences.

The red shoes represented Steven's inexhaustible desires, matched by my inexhaustible need to fulfill them. This dance was not a partnership, a mutual give and take, or a coordinated counterpoint—it was an obsession, an unhealthy fixation, and a death wish. I was not dancing out of love; I was dancing out of fear. At first, I was oblivious to the fact that it was not me who was doing the dance, but the shoes were dancing me. I longed for and admired the captivating red slippers— but these were no ruby slippers, ultimately taking me home. These bewitching red shoes took hold and would not let go, and their spell-binding pirouettes and fancy footwork (which inspired wonder, at first) became a nightmare.

I could relate. Once the young woman in the story realized she could not stop dancing (and that she could not remove the shoes), she was horrified. Out of panic and exhaustion, she begged the executioner to chop off her feet. It is a paradoxical twist when an executioner becomes a savior—when a violent severing is what is needed for healing to take place. However, that is how it is: sometimes pain must be endured in order to prevent a fate worse than death. Some part of ourselves must be sacrificed in order for us to live and thrive. For the young woman, her feet were that sacrifice—those shoes absolutely were going to dance her to death. Likewise, my own frantic desire to provide for all of Steven's wants and needs was like that hellish dance. Could it be that Richard served as my executioner, putting an end to my manic pursuit of Steven's love and acknowledgement?

In the story, once the amputation took place (shoes and all), the feet continued on, dancing off into the countryside. She, on the other hand, remained forever maimed by the executioner's axe. Her scars became a reminder of the price of striving. I felt as if some hideous part of me was still strapped into those shoes dancing off to parts unknown, leaving me with nothing but bloody stumps. That maniacal dance was the dance of the dark mother; her seductive beckoning compelled me to strive endlessly, fostering a distorted belief that fear and love were conjoined.

The death dance and shocking dismemberment were not the end of the story. In Estés' version, the girl lived on; she was older and wiser, and she overcame the need to strive for validation. In Anderson's tale, the young woman was finally escorted to heaven by an angel, where she was no longer burdened by her missing limbs. There, she knew eternal peace. Freed from her craving for love and acknowledgement, she was fulfilled.

At this point in the cycle of my relationship with my son, I have found a certain peace. I am continually transformed by living grief. Now, for the first time I feel free to experience life and embrace love every day. For too long, I did not believe that was possible—worse yet, I made sure it wasn't by wrapping myself in my suffering, searching every day for evidence of its presence, and finding ways to punish myself. That is what fueled my personal death dance.

So, when the calls from Steven no longer came like clockwork, I could have blamed Richard (or the CARE team) for taking away what was the one remaining connection I had with my son. To be honest, there was a time when I would have done just that. However, I now accept that all of the scurrying to fill orders, the questing to locate items on

Steven's wish list, not only left me feeling exhausted and empty, but it was a poor substitute for a relationship. My compulsion to strive for his acknowledgement came from my need to reaffirm our bond, and if I am to be completely honest, to feel validated as a mother—to prove that I wasn't a failure.

I am fully aware of the kinds of death the Mother/s Odyssey demands, and I know the pain of dismemberment. I have hung on the hook in the Underworld, like Inanna, and I have been resuscitated by angels. At times, despair and fury destroyed my will to go on just as it did for Demeter. Yet, I have been healed by the irreverent laughter of the crone—and today, I invite her more and more to take her place alongside the dark mother. Mary's serene gaze is no longer a mystery. I understand how one can live a peaceful life even while carrying those bloody swords. Myths and stories prove that living grief means accepting the never-ending cycles that propel one forward into a new way of being in the world—the way of bittersweet acceptance and mad joy.

EPILOGUE

In the end, my grief is not gone. In fact, in some ways, it is like an underground spring—a limitless supply of emotion—but, it no longer feels like an expanding void. For so long, I tried to protect myself from that void, because it was a trigger for striving, for climbing on the endless treadmill of condemnation and punishment. But I no longer wear the red shoes; I have stopped trying to prove that Steven's schizoaffective disorder is not my fault.

I still find it difficult to write to my son. I suppose it's because writing is my way of working through the emotions inherent in the Mother/s Odyssey. Writing is what allowed me to find meaning in the seeming meaningless of mental illness. Penning letters to Steven feels like throwing pieces of my soul over the edge of a cliff. If I'm not careful, the looming abyss can lead me straight back to the red shoes, luring me into frenetic emotional gyrations, and the dark mother will dance me straight to hell. I suppose this book is one long letter to my sons; one I hope will provide them with some comfort as they experience their own living grief, as we all do. Perhaps, I can share with them what all of my mythic and earthly teachers have shown me. If we are to come through our Mother/s Odysseys, we will be required to look closely at all aspects of ourselves and integrate them into our experience, and we'll need to *feel* all of the emotions we have tried so hard to deny.

So, fear comes and goes. Rage comes and goes. Despair comes and goes. Indeed, living grief gives me definition, but I am not defined by it. It does allow me to speak a common language with those who are on their Mother/s Odysseys. So many of them have come, offering companionship, healing, and support: a divine ambassador, a role model, a muse, a guide. Whatever role they served, they helped me to remember that even though living grief is lonely, I am not alone. They taught me to allow the cycle to play out naturally, to hope and despair, to rage and recover, to sacrifice and to celebrate. Sarah's presence forged in the fire of loss, and the lessons she lived, for example, were a treasure on my dark passage: this breath, this moment, this cup of coffee was enough. Strangely, I never heard from Sarah after I left the island. Now, I wonder, did I imagine her?

My Underworld experience in Hawai'i was the passage I needed to reconcile my grief, to integrate it more fully, and to come through transformed. On the island, I was immersed in the depths of my sorrow, anger, and fear with no filter, no "out," no distractions. By facing what I had spent decades avoiding, controlling, and suppressing, something shifted. For the first time, I have joy in a way that I previously could not. I did not plan for it or expect it, but this newly discovered joy is with me every day. It is not joy in spite of grieving; this mad joy, like a lotus, emerges out of the murky depths of living grief.

It has been ten years since the wild ride in Steven's convertible, when he shared his own joy and freedom, when he helped me to discover a desire for my own. In honor of that day, I head to the shore in my 1994 Geo Tracker—with the top down, and Rod Stewart belting *Forever Young* on the radio. This crazy little car is my third convertible since that transformative day in Kansas, before schizophrenia took my son from me. But now, I have come into a clearing on my grief passage. I see and appreciate the view. With the sun on my face and the wind in my hair, my heart is full. Grief, my familiar companion, rides shotgun. Stewart's lyrics fill the car, and tears pool in my eyes. Singing into the wind, it's okay. Today, I am at peace.

BIBLIOGRAPHY

Ayers, Mary Y. *Masculine Shame: From Succubus to the Eternal Feminine*, New York: Routledge, 2011.

Campbell, Joseph. *The Hero with a Thousand Faces*, Novato, CA: New World Library, 2008.

Beauvoir, Simone de. *The Second Sex*, New York: Vintage Books, 1989.

Eck, Diana L. *Darśan: Seeing the Divine Image in India*, New York: Columbia University Press, 1998.

Eliade, Mircea. *Rites and Symbols of Initiation*, New York: Harper and Row, 1975.

Estés, Clarissa Pinkola. *Women Who Run with Wolves*, London: Rider, 1992.

Frank, Jaffa Vernon. *The Eyes of the Gorgon: Endometriosis, Mythic Embodiment, and Freedom,* Sacramento, CA: Mandorla Books, 2019.

Freud. Sigmund. "On the Universal Tendency to Debasement in the Sphere of Love," in *The Standard Edition of the Complete Psychological Works of Sigmund Freud*, 11, trans. James Strachey, The Hogarth Press and the Institute of Psycho-Analysis, 1957.

Gaiman, Neil. *Norse Mythology*, New York: W.W. Norton & Co., 2017.

"Hávamál: The Words of Odin the High One," edited by D. L. Ashliman, *The Elder or Poetic Edda*, commonly known as *Sæmund's Edda, part I: The Mythological Poems*, edited and translated by Olive Bray, London: Viking Club, 1908, accessed: December 12, 2018, https://www.pitt.edu/~dash/havamal.html.

Hamilton, Edith. "Demeter (Ceres)," *Mythology: Timeless Tales of Gods and Heroes*, New York: Warner Books, 1942.

Hassett, Maurice. "Martyr," *The Catholic Encyclopedia,* vol. 9., New York: Robert Appleton Company, 1910, accessed July 30, 2020, http://www.newadvent.org/cathen/09736b.htm.

Holweck, Frederik. "Feasts of the Seven Sorrows of the Blessed Virgin," *The Catholic Encyclopedia*, New York: Robert Appleton Company, 1912, accessed August 12, 2020, https://www.newadvent.org/cathen/14151b.htm.

Jung, C.G. "Aion: Phenomenology of the Self." *The Portable Jung*, translation R.F.C. Hull, edited by Joseph Campbell, New York: The Viking Press, 1971.

Morford, Lenardon, and Sham. *Classical Mythology*, Oxford UP, accessed: December 12, 2018, https://global.oup.com/us/companion.websites/9780195397703/student/materials/chapter15/.

Roten, S.M., Father Johann. "Seven Joys of Mary Devotion," International Marian Research Institute. University of Dayton, Accessed: January 2, 2020. https://udayton.edu/imri/mary/s/seven-joys-of-mary-devotion php.

"Suicide, Anticlea, *The Odyssey*, 1997." Brean Brean, YouTube, Dec. 2, 2017, Video, https://www.youtube.com/watch?v=m5CP8psdkVo.

The Odyssey of Homer. Translated by Richmond Lattimore, Harper Perennial Modern Classics, 2007. https://issuu.com/bouvard6/docs/homer_s_odyssey__lattimor _.

Slattery, Dennis Patrick . *The Wounded Body: Remembering the Markings of Flesh*, NY: SUNY Press, 2000.

NOTES

[1] Joseph Campbell, *The Hero with a Thousand Faces* (Novato, CA: New World Library, 2008), 23. My ideas are heavily influenced by Campbell's "hero's journey," wherein the hero "ventures forth from the world of common day into a region of supernatural wonder; fabulous forces are . . . encountered and a decisive victory is won; the hero comes back from this mysterious adventure with the power to bestow boons" on others (23). Campbell divides the hero's journey into three main phases: separation, initiation, and return. In the separation phase it is common for the hero to receive the "call to adventure," which takes them away from the comforts of their familiar life and community (41).

[2] Dennis Patrick Slattery. *The Wounded Body: Remembering the Markings of Flesh* (NY: SUNY Press, 2000), 237.

[3] Jaffa Vernon Frank. *The Eyes of the Gorgon: Endometriosis, Mythic Embodiment, and Freedom* (Sacramento, CA: Mandorla Books, 2019), 1.

[4] Campbell, *The Hero with a Thousand Faces*, 88-90. Campbell suggests that a hero (or traveler on their passage) "whether god or goddess, man or woman, the figure in a myth, or the dreamer of a dream, discovers and assimilates his opposite . . . resistances are broken. . . . The ordeal is a deepening . . . the question is still in balance: Can the ego put itself to death?" (89).

[5] Edith Hamilton, "Demeter (Ceres)," *Mythology: Timeless Tales of Gods and Heroes* (New York: Warner Books, 1942), 50-55. My retelling is loosely based on Hamilton's version.

[6] Frederik Holweck, "Feasts of the Seven Sorrows of the Blessed Virgin," *The Catholic Encyclopedia*, (New York: Robert Appleton Company, 1912), accessed August 12, 2020, https://www.newadvent.org/cathen/14151b.htm. Catholic traditions commemorate Mary's seven sorrows with feasts: "The

object of these feasts is the spiritual martyrdom of the Mother of God and her compassion with the sufferings of her Divine Son."

[7] Maurice Hassett, "Martyr." *The Catholic Encyclopedia.* Vol. 9. (New York: Robert Appleton Company), 1910, accessed July 30, 2020. http://www.newadvent.org/cathen/09736b.htm. The number of "joys" (sometimes five, sometimes seven) varies depending on religious traditions.

[8] The number of "joys" (sometimes five, sometimes seven) varies depending on religious traditions.

[9] Father Johann Roten, S.M., "Seven Joys of Mary Devotion," (International Marian Research Institute. University of Dayton), accessed: January 2, 2020. https://udayton.edu/imri/mary/s/seven-joys-of-mary-devotion.php.

[10] *The Odyssey of Homer.* Translated by Richmond Lattimore, Harper (Perennial Modern Classics, 2007), accessed: December 12, 2018, https://issuu.com/bouvard6/docs/homer_s_odyssey__lattimore_. My telling here is loosely based on Lattimore's version unless otherwise stated.

[11] Morford, Lenardon, and Sham, *Classical Mythology.* (Oxford UP), accessed: December 12, 2018. https://global.oup.com/us/companion.websites/9780195397703/student/materials/chapter15/. According to Morford, Lenardon, and Sham's *Classical Mythology*, "Odysseus' meeting with his mother, ANTICLEA [an-ti-klay'a or an-ti-kleye'a], or ANTIKLEIA, is of the greatest importance; from her he learns about the mystery of existence." Therefore, Odysseus is like a "resurrection god, experiences the afterlife, and returns to this world, knowing with certainty the ultimate truth about life and death." Upon their meeting Anticlea reveals: "This is the doom of mortals when they die, for no longer do sinews hold bones and flesh together, but the mighty power of blazing fire consumes all, as soon as the life breath leaves our white bones and flesh, and the soul like a dream flutters and flies away."

[12] "Suicide, Anticlea, *The Odyssey*, 1997." YouTube, uploaded by Brean Brean, December 2, 2017.

[13] Neil Gaiman, *Norse Mythology*, (New York: W.W. Norton & Co. 2017), 21-22.

[14] Clarissa Pinkola Estés, *Women Who Run with Wolves*, (London: Rider, 1992), 365-66.. The author defines the term "descansos" as "symbols that mark a death." For example, the crosses one sees on the side of the road are markers that indicate where a life has been lost. Descansos are also burial grounds, according to Estés.

[15] "Hávamál: The Words of Odin the High One," edited by D. L. Ashliman, *The Elder or Poetic Edda*, commonly known as *Sæmund's Edda, part I: The Mythological Poems*, edited and translated by Olive Bray, (London: Printed for the Viking Club), 1908, 61-111, accessed June 26, 2019, https://www.pitt.edu/~dash/havamal.html. This is a translation of the original text from which my version is based.

[16] Simone de Beauvoir, *The Second Sex* (New York: Vintage Books, 1989) 670-1. St. Teresa's experience brings her a kind of sacred knowledge, as well as "intimacy" with the Divine. Beauvoir describes Teresa of Avila's account of penetration by a divine spear: "The angel held a long golden dart in his hands. From time to time he plunged it into my heart and forced it into my entrails" (670). Embedded in her account is the pairing of pain and pleasure, which elaborates the eroticism of ecstatic experience. "When he withdrew the dart, it was as if he were going to tear out my entrails, and it left me all inflamed with love divine" (670). St. Teresa insinuates marital intimacy in her encounter with the Divine: "I am certain that the pain penetrated my deepest entrails and it seemed as if they were torn when my spiritual spouse withdrew the arrow with which he had penetrated them" (670-1).

[17] Note that while individuals were present at Jesus' crucifixion, according to scripture, it is said that Jehovah turned his back on his son in his final hours. This represents the ultimate isolation.

[18] Diana L. Eck, *Darśan: Seeing the Divine Image in India*, (New York: Columbia University Press, 1998), 3-11. Eck describes *darśan*: "The central act of Hindu worship, from the point of view of the lay person, is to stand in the presence of the deity and to behold the image with one's own eyes, to see and be seen by the deity" (3). Eck points to the inherent relationship and reciprocity in this encounter. "Since, in the Hindu understanding, the deity is present in the image, the visual apprehension of the image is charged with religious meaning. Beholding the image is an act of worship, and through the eyes one gains the blessings of the divine" (11).

[19] C.G. Jung. "Aion: Phenomenology of the Self." In *The Portable Jung*, translation R.F.C. Hull, edited by Joseph Campbell, 139-162, (New York: The Viking Press, 1971). Jung's admittedly dated and gendered perspective asserted certain aspects of the mother archetype that represent "indescribable fulfillment," which is the "projection-making factor," that is dissolved when one realizes that in the realm of the psyche there is an image not only of the mother, but of a variety of feminine aspects: daughter, sister, lover, goddess, and the chthonic Baubo (or dark mother). Therefore, all feminine representations are "forced to become the carrier and embodiment of this omnipresent and ageless image, which corresponds to the deepest reality in man," according to Jung (150). In her idealized status "she stands for the loyalty, which in the interests of life he must sometimes forgo; [and] she is the much needed compensation for the risks, struggles, sacrifices that all end in disappointment; she is the solace for all the bitterness of life" (150). And yet, for Jung's everyman, she is also "the great illusionist, the seductress, who draws him into . . . not only life's reasonable and useful aspects, but into its frightful paradoxes and ambivalences where good and evil, success and ruin, hope and despair counterbalance one another (150).

[20] Mary Y. Ayers, *Masculine Shame: From Succubus to the Eternal Feminine* (New York: Routledge, 2011), 42. An example of an overt criticism of Freud shows up when Ayers stresses what she defines as Freud's "absurd interpretation" of nurture and bonding, in that he determined the longing for oneness with the father as an infant's primary drive, ignoring the innate connection between mother and child; she argues it is "as if Freud evacuates his deepest shame onto the mother, who becomes the contaminated person to be quarantined, isolated and forgotten as much as possible" (42). While one could say that this theory is supported by a collective disavowal of the mother, it must be noted that Ayers' critique is considered by some to lack substantive evidence.

[21] Mircea Eliade, *Rites and Symbols of Initiation* (New York: Harper and Row, 1975), 8-9.

[22] Slattery, Dennis Patrick. *The Wounded Body: Remembering the Markings of Flesh*, (NY: SUNY Press, 2000), 3-9.

[23] Slattery, *The Wounded Body*, 7.

[24] Mircea Eliade, *Rites and Symbols of Initiation*, 30.

[25] Dennis Patrick Slattery, *The Wounded Body,* (New York: SUNY Press, 2000), 15.

[26] Ibid, 238.

[27] Sigmund Freud. "On the Universal Tendency to Debasement in the Sphere of Love," in *The Standard Edition of the Complete Psychological Works of Sigmund Freud* 11, trans. James Strachey (The Hogarth Press and the Institute of Psycho-Analysis, 1957), 183. The dichotomous view of mothers and mothering ("good" and "bad") is reminiscent of Freud's assertions about the frustrated sexual desire for the mother, wherein the boy child (in this specific case study) must "degrade the mother to the level of prostitute" as a way of mitigating the incest taboo; "debasing the mother" reduces her to the desired "object of sensuality" (183). This fundamental psychoanalytic view underpins how Western psychology has traditionally perpetuated the Madonna/Whore complex Freud was working at.

[28] Edith Hamilton, "The Royal House of Thebes," in *Mythology: Timeless Tales of Gods and Heroes* (New York: Warner Books, 1999) 266-8. Dionysus was angry with his aunts (Agave, Ino, Autonoë), because in his view, they maligned his mother after her (Semele's) death. He cursed each of them, and they in turn experienced a mother's most profound grief, losing a child.

[29] Ibid, 267.

Made in the USA
Middletown, DE
05 February 2021